My Helicopter Sunday

– IAN STEWART –

20% off the profits made from this book will be donated to the
Rangers Supporters ERSKINE Appeal

BURGESS PUBLISHING
GLASGOW, SCOTLAND

HELICOPTER SUNDAY STORIES
Copyright © Ian Stewart 2009

All rights reserved.

No part of this book may be reproduced in any form by photocopying or any electronic or mechanical means, including information storage or retrieval systems, without permission in writing from both the copyright owner and the publisher of the book.

First published 2009 by
BURGESS PUBLISHING
Glasgow, Scotland.

Printed by
www.printondemand-worldwide.com

Thank You

To Iain Cathcart and Natasha McNicol for their kind permission to use their pictures.

To my long suffering wife Yvonne for tolerating my 'Magnificent Obsession' (particularly astonishing considering she favours the darkside)

To my dear old father Jackie, the fallings out over the Rangers have got less frequent over the years, but the passion burns just as fiercely, I will be forever grateful .

To my Mother Dunena the best referee in the business.

To the kiddywinkles, one out of five favouring the darkside is not too bad a legacy.

Lastly, sincere thanks to all the fans who kindly shared their experiences with us.

Introduction

My earliest memory of following Rangers is not a happy one. It is a dreich, dank late-April afternoon and from the bay window of my aunt Lily's top floor flat in Airlie Street, Hyndland I am watching my father return crestfallen from the 1969 Scottish Cup Final. There have been many occasions since that I have felt the same raw disappointment as my father. However, these have been far outweighed by the success and happy days that follow following Rangers for over 40 years has brought me.

My father I have to thank for the introduction to and instilling in me the love of football and Rangers Football Club in particular. It was not, though, till I was around 8 that I took a real interest, much to my father's undoubted relief.

My first match was a bit of a disappointment as it was a 2-0 home defeat by Aberdeen in September 1971. My abiding memory of the match was the first sight of the lush green turf coming into view in the bright afternoon sunshine the singing and then the crushing disappointment that the Gers wore white socks. That explained the defeat to an eight-year-old – they didn't look like Rangers! Ever since then, other than the dark days of the early eighties, it has been pretty much success all the way.

Over this time I had a few heroes, some obvious, others less so; Derek Parlane, Alex MacDonald, Stewart Kennedy, Davie Cooper, Terry Butcher, John Brown and the absolute daddy of them all The Prince of Denmark - Brian Laudrup. I have witnessed many memorable matches. My favourites being a 3-0 trashing of Celtic in January 1975 (my first Old Firm game), the 2-0 win over Dinamo Kiev in 1987, the nine-man 2-2 draw with Celtic the same year, and the Michael Mols inspired 4-1 win over PSV Eindhoven in 1999.

The early years of the 21st century have, though, been trying times. I have watched our stranglehold on the game in Scotland eroded by a resurgent Celtic. The problems our club has encountered, many self-inflicted, have been painful to watch but the failure to succeed against O'Neill's (and then Strachan's) Celtic have caused the most angst. It was therefore what appeared to be the shape of life as we knew it when Celtic came to Ibrox on 24th April 2005 and won 2-1 putting them 5 points ahead with only four games left, that the League was gone for another year.

My father and I left Ibrox that day with that 'dank dreich April' feeling again. We were told to keep believing by Big Marvin but honestly the vast majority of follow followers surely thought this was simply 'playing to the gallery', paper talk - oh, us of little faith!

There has to my mind been nothing to beat the dramatic events experienced by every Ranger across the globe, at Easter Road, in their house, pub or club than the events of 22nd May 2005. That it was so totally unexpected, the timing of the unfolding events at Fir Park and Easter Road and the sheer and utter unbridled joy it released, along of course with the added 'get it right up ye' factor that it inflicted on our greatest rivals, was the absolute icing on the cake.

Each and every supporter has a tale to tell of how the joy of the events manifested itself. There are many, they are varied, they are worth sharing. Some are laugh-out-loud funny, some truly poignant, but in my humble opinion they all convey what it feels like to be a football supporter and follow truly the greatest club in the world.

The pages of this book are the records of these tales. The language is as presented by the contributors so is not without expletives and in places not for the faint-hearted! Thank you to all who agreed they could be shared. Some names attributed to the stories are user names from the *Follow Follow* message board.

You are our club. You are what makes us 'More than a club' and shows the world truly 'We are the people'. I hope you enjoy reading them as much as I did.

Setting the Scene

The 2004/05 season had been nip and tuck all the way. The last Old Firm meeting on 24th April would have a crucial bearing. Positions before the game were as follows:

		P	W	D	L	F	A	PTS	G/D
Celtic		33	27	2	4	77	28	83	+49
Rangers		33	25	6	2	67	17	81	+50

Rangers having home advantage were slight favourites. The game was an unmitigated disaster from Rangers' perspective as they were well and truly horsed. Simply unable to contain Craig Bellamy, who it has to be said scored a quite stunning individual goal. The Copland Road were also very sporting in that when Stan Petrov scored the opening goal they obligingly passed him on a wee cup of Coke to thank him for his efforts.

Celtic had several chances to kill the game totally but Stevie Thompson gave Rangers a glimmer of hope with a goal two minutes from time. This, however, just added to the general discontent and disgruntlement me and my father felt leaving Ibrox in resignation that we had blown it. And the table told the following sorry tale:

		P	W	D	L	F	A	PTS	G/D
Celtic		34	28	2	4	79	29	86	+50
Rangers		34	25	6	3	68	19	81	+49

Saturday 30th April 2005

Celtic being, incredibly, surprisingly generous decided to let Hibs hump them 3-1 at home; suddenly the title race had been re-ignited.

The net result of this stroke of good fortune was a blazing barney between me and my father. Him on the basis we were a useless shower for not winning the week before and now being in a position to put Celtic to the sword; me for pointing out that this simply proved Celtic weren't actually a very good team. It was one of those arguments where we both were probably right but neither of us was prepared to back down. My mother was left to play the Kofi Annan role.

Sunday 1ˢᵗ May 2005

In torrential rain we went to Pittodrie, not a particularly happy hunting ground for us, and I prepared for a gut-wrenching ninety minutes. Second pleasant surprise of the weekend duly arrived as we were comfortable 3-1 winners inspired by a superb performance from Dado Pršo.

League Standings:

		P	W	D	L	F	A	PTS	G/D
Celtic		35	28	2	5	80	32	86	+48
Rangers		35	26	6	3	71	20	84	+51

Saturday 7ᵗʰ May 2005

We are the Saturday game this time, against Hearts. This was a game where we were made to sweat after being comfortably 2-0 ahead through Thomas Buffel and Marvin Andrews. As the game is trudging towards its conclusion Big Marv decides to make things interesting by belting one into his own net. This leads to a nerve-shredding final nine minutes but we get there in the end and return to the summit for one day at least.

Sunday 8ᵗʰ May 2005

Until this season the Celtic/Aberdeen fixture has been almost a 'gimme' for Celtic. In the preceding few years the Dons sought ever more timid ways of capitulating. Aberdeen had turned this round by winning two of the last three fixtures at Parkhead. Could they do it again? While we hoped, I think every Rangers supporter knew deep down how this would unfold. As it transpired, Aberdeen made Celtic work and kept things level at the interval. But a minute after the restart Celtic were ahead through Hartson, and in seventy-one minutes the same player clinched the points.

Revised League Standings:

	P	W	D	L	F	A	PTS	G/D
Celtic	36	29	2	5	82	32	89	+50
Rangers	36	27	6	3	73	21	87	+51

Saturday 14th May 2005

We have a Saturday game again and a chance to return to the top and put Celtic under pressure. Though what was shaping up to be a tricky fixture for them at Tynecastle was diminished somewhat by the departure of Hearts manager John Robertson in the week leading up to the game.

Anyway that was for the following day and all Rangers could do was do their own job. We duly deliver in thumpingly convincing fashion, running all over a woeful Motherwell side. Shota Arveladze signs off on his farewell appearance at Ibrox with a couple of well taken goals, ably assisted by a double from Thomas Buffel. Big Marv, while telling us to keep believing, keeps forgetting which way he is shooting and scores in his own net for the second week running.

While we all depart with a warm glow, the flipside is how on earth can a team as poor as Motherwell were today hope to trouble Celtic next Sunday?

Sunday 15th May 2005

Could not bear to watch Hearts v Celtic on the bizarre basis that if I don't view it then when I go to find out the score I will get a huge surprise - explain that logic to me? In the end Celtic scrape home after an opening goal from Alan Thompson which was deflected past Craig Gordon. Hearts equalised on 71 minutes through Paul Hartley but six minutes later substitute Craig Beattie won the day for Celtic.

It appeared to be the general consensus, and certainly mine, that Celtic had cleared the last real hurdle between them and the Championship, and no one could see them not closing matters out the following Sunday.

League positions going into final weekend:

		P	W	D	L	F	A	PTS	G/D
Celtic		37	30	2	5	84	33	92	+51
Rangers		37	28	6	3	77	22	90	+55

Sunday 22nd May 2005

The Helicopter Changes Direction

This was a strange day as I awoke with no expectations and contemplated not actually watching either game. My recently-pregnant wife Yvonne was suffering the literal gut-wrenching early days of child expectancy, and being a supporter of the dark side had decided early on to anticipate prematurely what every Septic supporter would be feeling some hours later.

So as she was in bed, it was on with the TV and the ultimate sadomasochism.

Easter Road – 4 mins: Garry O'Connor goes close for Hibs as Ronnie the Perm beats out his 25-yarder.

Easter Road – 9 mins: O'Connor again, this time just too high with a header.

Easter Road – 10 mins: Hibs keeper Brown completely misjudges a through ball and Novo is presented with an open goal but only succeeds in hitting the inside of the post. This is how it is all going to end – feck!

Easter Road - 25 mins: Novo hits the side netting with a 20-yarder.

Fir Park – 29 mins: Sutton scores. Cue resignation, the miracle was not going to happen.

Easter Road - 35 mins: Buffel from 16 yards after being played in by Rae hits it straight at Brown in the Hibs goal.

Easter Road - 48 mins: Goal-saving tackle from Caldwell.

Easter Road - 51 mins: Murray makes a mistake to let in Buffel who makes a complete hash of the opportunity.

Easter Road - 58 Mins: Buffel sets up Novo whose shot is helped into the net by Celtic-bound Caldwell. At last! At least we are going to go out with a win.

Easter Road from 58 mins on: After you Claude!

Fir Park - 88 mins: Scott McDonald strikes a dagger into Celtic's heart with an over-the-shoulder hooked shot.

Easter Road – 88 mins: Unbridled joy!

Living room in sunny Southside Glasgow – commencement of impending lunatic behaviour.

Fir Park - 90 mins: Just to rub salt into the gaping chasm of a wound, 2-1 The Well - Get in there Skippy!

Easter Road - 90 mins: Delirium

All the Rangers bars, clubs, houses etc. – We have lift off and here are the tales!

Ian Stewart

Their Helicopter Sunday Days

Ian Stewart

Otisblue

'Watched' Helicopter Sunday unfold on the BBC text page here in Canada, before the days of LFO, switching between BBC and *Follow Follow*. Then someone posted that McDonald (whom I had never heard of) had scored at Fir Park. Didn't know who he played for, if it was Motherwell or a Celtic reserve. It all started to click when the old board went into meltdown. Unbelievable how the emotion can get hold of you even watching text on a computer screen.

Tom McClure

Came home from Cyprus that morning and at Glasgow airport there were two mhankies in full green 'n' grey with 'Champions 2005' on the back. Oh how I chuckled later on that day. It still makes me smile to this day, them in the air thinking they'd won, then picture their faces when they get to their resort and reality smacks them between the eyes.

Derek Harper

I have got a cardboard Bank of Scotland SPL trophy which Barry Ferguson launched into the crowd - it's up on the hall wall and greets visitors. I am also on the DVD, at the final whistle.

Stuart Smith

I remember after Helicopter Sunday most of the players came into The District Bar, and as they were leaving to get on their bus they were doing pics and signing autographs. I saw Pršo and went over to get my picture taken with him. As my girlfriend and I ran over, she tripped and badly smashed her face on the ground. I missed my picture opportunity but the laugh of it was she tried to blame the 'stupid kerb' for tripping her up. Nothing to do with the fact we had drunk all day in the pub.

Helicopter Sunday by Brian MacKechnie

Let me tell you the tale of a Sunday in May,
We were two points behind Celtic with one game to play.
The tims had been crowing " the title's in the bag,
We've won the league again, fly the flag, fly the flag. "
They would be taught a lesson they'll always remember,
Don't write off the Rangers, we never surrender.

We descended on Leith on the 22nd of May,
The waiting was over, it was judgement day.
With hope in our hearts and trannies in our hands,
We packed ourselves into the Easter Road stands.

The ref blew the whistle, the action began,
A wave of excitement swept over the fans.
But half an hour in came the news we were dreading,
Chris Sutton had scored, for 2nd place we were heading.

Soon half-time arrived and our score remained zero,
We looked to the heavens and prayed for a hero.
The teams re-emerged and the second half started,

My Helicopter Sunday

Not one of our loyal fans had departed.

Then all of a sudden - a promising break,
Tam Buffel to Novo, who made no mistake.
1-0 to the Rangers, we were off the mark,
Our attentions now turned to events at Fir Park.

Ra' Celtic were coasting as the minutes ticked by,
They sang Championees and the Fields of Athenry.
But you and I know there was a sting in the tail,
For theirs is a club which is destined to fail.

Enter Scott MacDonald with an overhead kick,
Rab Douglas is nowhere and Timmy is sick.
Their fans were despondent and looked to the skies,
But there was no solace there for their tear-stained eyes.

For a helicopter was approaching the ground,
But it wasn't descending, it was turning around.
Over on the touchline, O'Neill lost the plot,
Astonishingly brilliant, I think fucking not!

Soon word reached Leith and the Rangers fans roared,
The players on the pitch knew that Motherwell had scored.
The players kept possession, we awaited more news,
Tension gripped all of the red, white & blues.

Then two minutes later - a heart warming sound,
Another eruption at our end of the ground.
2-1 to Motherwell and it had to be him,
MacDonald again, not bad for a Tim!

The final whistle sounded and the copter arrived,

This time it was landing with the SPL prize.
Strangers hugged strangers up and down the land,
As the words KEEP BELIEVING appeared in the stand

The singing began - " Cheer up Marty,
Come over to our place, we're having a party. "
And over at Ibrox, though minutes had passed,
A sea of red, white & blue had amassed.

Hundreds of bears lined Edmiston Drive,
The team bus arrived and the place came alive.
The party continued well into the night,
A reward for a season of courage and fight.

And I urge fellow bears to take heed of this rhyme,
As we find ourselves now in more difficult times.
Protest if you must at the current regime,
But unite on a Saturday and get behind the team.

When you're finding it hard to muster belief,
Think back to that day when the sun shone on Leith.
'Cos like the moon landings and JFK,
We'll always remember that Sunday in May.
The odds were against us but we won the race,
Let the others come after us, we welcome the chase.

Garry Lynch

I went straight back to Ibrox after Easter Road and there was a young couple sat behind me with a baby of four months old who was enthralled with the noise and the things going on around him. I gave my ticket stub to his dad and told him it would help the kid remember his first visit to Ibrox. Great memories indeed.

Cammy

I watched the match at my dad's with my brother, uncle, mother etc. The wife was listening on the radio at home and the phone rang an instant before the second goal at Motherwell came through Setanta. As soon as it rang I knew we had won it.

On the way home driving through Uddingston I saw their buses coming, heading for the 'party' at Parkheid. This was the 'suits' who had paid probably £400 for the day. Their faces said it all.

Scott Kerr

Still remember it like it was yesterday. Watching us on the big screen in the Corona and the barman keeping us updated on events at Fir Park. Cue scenes of joy, much leaping around and getting sprayed with bubbly from the bar staff!

Then heading over to Ibrox and seeing guys in taxis with carry-oots. Everybody was singing all the way up to Ibrox and then we saw the bus coming back from Edinburgh with the players onboard!

The sun shone and the party carried on!

Fuckin' amazin' day!

Adam Sneddon

Sat in the Hibs end trying to fake an Edinburgh accent. Helicopter Sunday was crap up until 88 minutes. Then trying not to react when we scored (tip: punching your legs and shouting, "Fuck" repeatedly convinces them you are a Hibee).

Afterwards? Singing *We are the Champions* in the Hibs

end with a tiny wee pocket of other Bears, before being told by a steward to leg it the second we got outside as there was a group 'waiting for us'.

The rest? A drunken and hugely enjoyable blur that ended about 1:30am. I was that hyper, I woke up early and went into work an hour early next morning, and straight to the pub again when I finished.

Craig Brown

By far the best day of my life. I'll never forget sitting in my cousin's house because I couldn't get a ticket and saying to him, "Well, we're winning here, you might as well turn it onto their game." (I don't know why I said that because usually I would have said, "Well I'm not sitting here watching them win the league.") He turned over and I'll never forget it.

"McDonald has scored for Motherwell. Scott MacDonald has scored for Motherwell."

I've never had a feeling like it, but once it all calms back down again you're thinking to yourself, these chunts will score. Then Motherwell break again.

"Give the ball to Patterson, give the ball to Paattt... aww for fuck sake! Yeeeessss!"

I thought the house was going to fall down, the amount of things that were broken, but no one cared.

The start of the biggest and longest party I've ever had. I was on study leave for my standard grades and I've never looked forward to going into school in my life never mind an exam but I did after that.

Jamie McFarlane

Possibly the best day of my life. The house 3 doors

down from us were having a Tims' championship-winning party (BBQ, drink, TV, house full of them). Oh how sweet it was to see their faces when they left the house after the 90 minutes! Brilliant!

Ewan Renfrew

The day before Helicopter Sunday I was watching my boy's team playing football. One of the other boy's dad comes over (Sellic Man) and he goes on about the Hearts game the previous week (Hearts denied penalty) and how it's about 'The Whole Season', not just one game. Couldn't wait till he'd finished to be honest, as he was trying to get a reaction.

The next Saturday was the boys' prize giving and I couldn't wait! I let him stew a bit and then wandered up to him when he was at the bar and said casually, "You were right you know, it is all about the whole season, not just one game!"

Alan Watt

Helicopter Sunday in the pub one of the Tims was having a title-winning party and gave us invitations for it at the start of the game. We took his champagne off him and soaked him, telling him he didn't need it now as his party was cancelled.

Anon

This was even better than Løvenkrands' goal in the

Scottish Cup Final. As soon as the second goal went in and the kick off was taken I phoned a Tim acquaintance to see where he was. And I told him to look for us on TV when he got home and he would see us in the singing and dancing end. He was raging.

Dave Raeburn

Think the Brazen Head takes some beating here. Ten minutes before the final whistle the Brazen were getting their 'Congratulations' banner ready to put above the pub. It reached the length of the pub.

The staff were putting the banner up when Motherwell scored, but continued to do so anyway. Being busy trying to finish getting the banner up they hadn't realised their new star had just scored another goal for Motherwell. Whilst standing back admiring their good work and taking some photos, there came the shouts from inside the pub, "Get that fuckin' thing down, Rangers are champions."

If only I could get a copy of their pictures.

Tommy Graham

Helicopter Sunday - when could a 50-year-old guy dance with one of his workmates in the middle of Mosspark Boulevard stopping traffic and get away with it. Also think that for the first time in ages we had people actually showing the allegiance to us that day.

Everywhere I looked were happy, smilcy faces, even old dears at the side of road.

Ian Stewart

Watched the last five minutes of their game as ours was

petering out - more in hope than expectation. Then old 'safe hands' (Rab Douglas) flapped at a corner and I thought, oh ho! When the equaliser went in I think the medical term for it is 'going absolutely berserk'. I had been nervously pacing about before and had actually washed the laminate floor in the living room. So in my state of 'berserkness' I jumped so high I hit my head on the living room ceiling, landed on the wet floor, fell on my arse and banged my head on the floor. Then I ran outside shouting, "Get it right up ye!" Returned to the house, flicked over to see the reaction at Easter road, flicked back to see Scott McDonald running away and thought they were replaying the equalizer only to then realise it was actually his second. Cue more lunatic behaviour(hardly befitting a man in his forties) including running up and down the stairs about ten times.

My father, who lives in Argyll, left the house at half-time in disgust. He is the most pessimistic pessimist you have ever met and couldn't bear to listen to it any longer. Anyway, there is a canal behind his house so he went for a ride on his bike to calm his rage. He met one of his Gers-supporting buddies on the canal bank in a similar frame of mind. They were both in the depths of despair when this bloke went by telling them we were champions. Cue a 70 and 45-year-old hugging and dancing about like a couple of ladyboys. Then a mad dash home on his bike, almost crashing into the canal at least half a dozen times, to be met with an answer machine message from now totally demented, out of control, oldest child shouting, "Ya fuckin' beauty!" down the phone.

The scenes at Easter Road after the final whistle and when the team came back out showed how much it really meant to the players. In fact it visibly showed that it truly meant as much to them, every single one of them, as it did to us lifelong supporters.

Cue up to the Brox and party time. Carry-outs openly being carried into the ground for the first time for possibly over 20 years and a general 'feeling ecstatic' kinda mood prevailing. Even the slightly curtailed celebrations were worth every precious second. Restaurant staff dancing in the Main Stand, and at the end Big Zorba in the Main Stand waving the Greek flag, gesturing to the Copland Stand and pointing to his heart. It would have brought a tear to a glass eye. The one thing it brought home to me was something I was not really sure existed – truly. This concept of the Rangers family that the Chairman always talks about. I have always thought the staff were one family and we were the slightly rowdy relations. However, Sunday 22nd May 2005 bonded us, the players and the management like, I think, no other time I can remember in 40 years of following the Bears.

I also witnessed an open, visible, tangible joy and celebration the likes of which I have not witnessed for a very long time. The scenes of fans standing out of sunroofs in cars and horns blaring along Paisley Road West will live with me for ever. This is what it must have been like on VE day. I am struggling to remember a better feeling - so unexpected, and with O'Neill quitting and seeing their despair, does it get any better?

We will all, I am sure, have witnessed the various supporters' video clips posted on YouTube. The guy in the grey jacket at Easter Road determined not to celebrate prematurely and keeping cool, then when the second goal goes in releasing all his joy. Superb! The clips from behind big Safe Hands' goal from the Well supporter – Yes Skippy! Yes Skippy! Yes. Priceless! The tears and looks of stunned disbelief from Fir Park – money could not buy that misery. Brilliant!

On the Monday following, in between Yvonne insisting on watching Coronation Street and other associated mince, I was flicking across to Rangers TV and Celtic TV who were replaying both games again. Anyway, do you know what the Celtic programme was called in the banner where you preview channels... *Champions Special*! Thing is guys, how on earth do you top that?

Jocky

We were all in the Rangers Club in Corby as we were going to have an end-of-season party anyway. I will never forget the feeling until my dying day of the coverage at Easter Road as the Hibs fans went quiet, the coverage switched to Fir Park and we all watched in awe as McDonald scored the goal. The club went absolutely ballistic. There were tears, cheers and plenty of beers. It took us 2 hours to find out that the Septic had actually been beaten 2-1. It is and always will be the best day of my life.

Mark Sheppard

A friend of mine was at sea watching the BBC online commentary when McDonald scored. He went fucking mental, shrieking and screaming. About half a dozen people rushed into his room thinking something was wrong. They finally managed to calm him down after a couple of minutes. He took a breath and was about to tell them what had happened when the second goal flashed up and set him off again.

Craig Burton

I was in the toilet in my da's and coming out heard the 10 or so people going mental downstairs. I started to run down the stairs before missing one and going headfirst down them. I'm lying at the bottom in agony as my auntie sticks her head round the door to shout up that Motherwell had scored. Then she looks down at me in a heap and says, "That's fuckin' 1–1 with the scum, get up off the floor you arsehole."

I limped in, in agony, sat down then the second goes in and the pain is forgotten.

Harrowblue

There was a christening in my local club in Harrow and I was over there paying lip service to all the Taigs when my mate phones me and tells me that Motherwell had equalised. I run home and climb into the loft and fish out the old 2-foot Tenerife cigar (I knew it would come in handy one day) and head back to the club in my Rangers top. A guy who was down from Scotland bought me drinks all day and we had a right good sing-song, tears and everything.

Bob Wilson

I was at sea, somewhere off the coast of Libya, and unable to receive any match details on BBC World Service. I received a little knock on my cabin door, with one of my Filipino crew looking confused with an Inmarsat fax for me from the missus. These faxes are usually reserved for death of cat / send me some money / you have won the lottery, due to the cost. This one said, 'McDonald has scored'. So straight on to GMDSS (the ship's radio) trying to get BBC or Radio Ulster (I jest not, you will be surprised where you can get Radio Ulster). Meanwhile more faxes arrived with continued updates.

Eventually I got a BBC News report about the whole situation and final result. Outcome - Rangers win League, I have a massive phone bill and company D & A policy suspended for evening.

Derek Brown

Swapped my shift that week so meant that I was working on the Sunday. So got up at 6am and picked the papers up on the way to my work, with the headlines on the back page about O'Neill leaving after Sunday's game. As soon as I read the headlines I had a feeling that we were going to do it. So as the day progressed a Timmy in my work kept on winding me and my fellow Bears up saying that we had no chance, blah, blah, blah.

The games kick off and we are surrounding my radio to hear the latest. Nothing to report apart from both of us are winning. Then in the last ten minutes Timmy is over listening to my radio with a smile on his face. Next, chaos as MacDonald scores. The Bears erupt and the adrenaline starts pumping and I am thinking, are we going to do this? Timmy's smile is quickly removed with McDonald scoring again. Me and the Bears start singing, jumping up and down and basically going mental.

I just couldn't work anymore. As soon as 7pm came I bombed it down the M8 to Ibrox to see the team. Met up with my dad and wee brother in the Govan as soon as the team came out. Just wish the fans kept off the park for a wee while longer. Then took my dad to the New Regent.

I went home and my pals came down and we drank the

night away watching the videos of Helicopter Sunday on YouTube. Only regret is that I had swapped my shift and wasn't in the pub to watch. But plenty of video footage to put a smile on my face for years to come. Nobody will ever forget Helicopter Sunday.

Scott Gemmel

Was at the match and I swear this is true. A few minutes to go and I had a look behind me (I was upper tier at the front) and imagined what it would be like if the whole place suddenly erupted. As I was doing so, the place did. I was stunned. Could not believe it. Starting half going mental and half trying to find out what the fuck had happened (obvious now, I know). Then it happened again, was ages before I realised that it was a second goal, most of us thought it was the final whistle.

Best day of my life. Didn't go back to Ibrox which I now regret but a storming night on the bevvy back down in the shire. As for work the next day... that's another story.

Finlay McLellan

I have Sky, but not Setanta.

My wife was having an afternoon nap with my (at the time) small baby boy (he'd been up all night crying and teething!)

Was flicking through the channels and ended up on Sky Sports News. There must have been about 10-15 minutes left and they were telling us that 'they' were 1-0 up as were we.

Oh well, I thought, that's it for another year.

Left the channel on and went to get a drink and then it came up with the *Goal Alert* banner. 2-0 to Septic, I thought, but was jumping for joy when they announced it was 1-1! Was trying my hardest not to scream in joy for fear of waking the wee fella up when it went 2-1 to Well, and we had won the league!

My neighbour downstairs and I were extremely happy. You couldn't wipe the smile off our faces with Brillo pads. The wife was happy too as she and the wee yin managed to get a good couple of hours sleep without me screaming like an idiot!

Martin H

A week before the game me and my pal Graeme ventured to the Rangers shop in Dumfries High Street as he wanted to buy the home shirt. He also decided to get Buffel 4 on the back of it. Unfortunately, the halfwits in the store printed it Buffell 4 (incorrect spelling). Anyway, this is sort of by the by. The day of the game we went back to the shop to get it changed and they obliged with a new top and the correct spelling.

Driving to the pub we drove past a guy in a Gers top walking his dog, this prompted Graeme to tell me he had a 'feeling about today'. Oh how he was correct!

We proceeded to the Riverside Bar to meet the rest of the boys and watch the game, well the first half anyway. Half-time came and me and my other pal Clarke took a quick trip into the town to get some much needed scran. Suddenly it was the second half and we dived into the nearest pub, JAY-KAY'S, only to discover they had the Motherwell-Celtic game on. Anyway, we sat and thankfully the barmaid flicked channels for us as she was 'one of them' and wanted to watch her team but, as they say, 'the customer is always right'!

Anyway, some might say that we should have left as soon as this happened but there were only three other people in the bar and as long as I was with my mate and the footy was on we didn't bother leaving. Then it happened. Sitting silent at the thought of Celtic lifting the title and having a smug barmaid behind the bar, in the dying minutes of the game up pops Scott McDonald with his first goal! We proceeded to go tonto in the bar and get right in the face of the barmaid. A quick sit down and we were at it again! Another goal for McDonald!

This time it was straight out the door and back to the Riverside to party with the rest of the Bluenoses! We parked the car about 200 yards from the bar and I can tell you this, I am a pretty big lump of a guy but you couldn't see me for dust as soon as the car door closed! 200 yards in a matter of seconds, then it was time to squeeze our way through the thick crowd of Bluenoses in the bar to get to the mates we left behind at half-time.

"It's 1-1! It's 1-1!" they were shouting at me.

"No it's no, it's 2-1!" was the reply.

The rest of the day/night is sort of hard to remember as it is a bit of a blur but I can promise you I will never, ever forget that day for the rest of my life! A day cemented in Rangers' history and etched in my memory.

Iain

Went to a works conference on the Wednesday before the game. Returned on the Saturday afternoon, watched the FA Cup Final and had a few beers. Spent the Sunday afternoon on *Follow Follow* listening to the game on the radio. I was resigned to the fact that the league was lost, and then I heard the crowd noise from Easter Road. For a few seconds I couldn't move and then when I realised what had happened I was jumping around my living room like a madman. This continued until the games had finished and then I went into shock.

Cameron Bell/Stuart Atkinson

Being in the Hall in Sauchiehall Street with my mate, as the Hall decided to show only the Rangers game, and O'Neill's next door were showing only the Celtic game.

I was the only person in the pub with a radio listening to Clyde on my mobile, a pissy Nokia number that had an even worse signal. I may also add at that point I had publicly declared on the *Follow Follow* message board that we WOULD NOT win the title. I was adamant in my opinion, so much so I ridiculed others for their misplaced belief 'they' could slip up so spectacularly.

In fact, I was so demotivated that I was just on time to see KO, and had to grab seats at the front of the screen to the left of the pub. So I was left listening to my mate gibbering, "What's happening?" every 2 minutes.

Dodgy Clyde commentary and dodgy Setanta commentary. When Sutton scored I threw my phone across the other side of the table and begrudgingly retrieved it when I had calmed down. Novo then scored and it was really strange, as I still felt the goal was redundant.

Then it happened. I heard Motherwell break, and then McDonald had scored and almost exactly at the same time it broke on Setanta. Cue a split-screen then a replay of the goal.

My mate and I went crazy alongside the rest of the pub, screaming and hugging each other. My mate, however, shouted at me to get back on the radio and keep listening. I was actually shaking every time Celtic were mentioned, and that tubby bastard Johnstone saying, "Celtic can still score," every two minutes like a handwringer prick. I was barely conscious of my mate still holding my arm, with his grip getting tighter every passing minute. When McDonald scored again I leapt about 18 feet in the air, screaming my head off, then turned around to the remainder of the pub, still looking at me in disbelief, and I clicked Setanta hadn't announced it!

I screamed, "It's facking 2-1 to Motherwell!" and the whole place went completely mental. Everybody was cheering championees and I nearly burst into tears.

When the full whistle came I nearly broke down, I was totally stunned. My mate just kept hugging me and I was just bewildered at what had happened. Then the guy who was sitting across from me picked me up, hugged me and said his girlfriend couldn't look at my face in case the filth had scored again!

Finished our drinks and went to the Brox for the party.

Listening even now to the Clyde commentary still sends shivers up my spine.

Davie Gray

My wee workmate decided to get a deal and head off to Spain for the weekend to get out of the way. He got friendly with a big Ulsterman and his wife and they decided to go and watch the game together. They go to a pub which was split 50/50.

As we all know, Sutton scored, Novo scored and the match got to about five minutes to go. The camera switches to Easter Road and it shows the Rangers fans with their heads in their hands.

At this point a Tim at the other end of the pub shouts

out, "Have a look at them sad orange bassas," and the big Ulsterman decides he can't listen to it anymore and leaves the pub with his wife.

About one hundred yards down the road he hears a roar [1-1], so he decides to pop back to see what happened. By the time he gets back to the pub McDonald has got his second and the cameras are back at Easter Road with the Bears going mental. The big Ulsterman walks over to the stage, turns on the microphone and says, "Would you have a look at them sad orange bassas now."

The Mickey side of the pub emptied.

Davie Watson

A little tale which happened after the event.

Sellic played in the Scottish Cup Final the next week, and that morning the local Sellic supporters bus held their AGM in the local pub which is run by my big mate (and a Tim). Got my son to phone and ask for his dad who was travelling on the bus with friends.

Just as the AGM began, cue one barman shouting, "Is there a Scott McDonald on the bus, Scott McDonald?" Two seconds of silence then uproar in the background.

"Fuck off ya Hun bastard." Phone slammed down.

Carlsberg don't do phone wind-ups but if they did…

Frank Gallagher

A friend and I travelled over from Carrickfergus, Northern Ireland on the Saturday night. We had arranged to stay with friends in Tarbolton, Ayrshire on the Saturday night and had booked the Travelodge on Paisley Road West for the Sunday night(just in case).

Having went to a local pub in Tarbolton on the

Saturday night I woke on the Sunday morning buzzing (don't ask me why). I got ready for the football and heard the horn beep outside my mate's house. There were about 8 of us going up so we hired a people carrier/minibus. When I looked out the window it was a bright yellow bus (known to this day as the yella vengabus).

Once we arrived at Easter Road the place was jumping – some people did believe. Then came the inevitable, they had scored at Motherwell which was cheered by the Hibs fans!

Our game trundled on until wee Nacho popped up and the Rangers end went crazy. Minutes later I was slumped in my seat, still realising that the goal meant nothing to us unless Motherwell could do something for us.

As I sat in my seat with minutes remaining the Rangers end went berserk. McDonald had scored. I couldn't watch our game. I stood and faced the other way. I remember saying to my mate, "The scum will score again, I know it!"

The next 4 minutes were the longest of my life. Then came the biggest cheer and outpouring of joy I have ever witnessed. Motherwell had made it 2-1, although I only found this out when we got back to the vengabus (I thought we were cheering the full-time whistle).

When we got back on board the vengabus you would expect the place to be going mad, it wasn't. There was hardly a word spoken until we got to Glasgow. We got dropped off at the District Bar and went in. Again the place seemed to be in disbelief. We stayed a while and then went to The Louden and The Clachan with a mate. When walking back to the District we noticed a large crowd gathered outside. I thought there must be a few players in there. When we got inside the majority of the first team were there.

Fergie was sitting by himself in the Front Bar. I asked, "Why are you not in with the rest of the boys?"

His reply, "I still can't believe this big chap."

What a night was had celebrating for a few hours with Dado, Big Boab, Andy Watson (who we enjoyed a wee sing-along with), Michael Ball, Graeme Smith, Ross McCormack to name a few.

No matter how much drink was taken that day (and the Monday) I will always remember that weekend as clear as day. WE ARE THE PEOPLE.

John Carroll

Having stopped travelling to away games a few years ago, I went with my usual routine of heading round to a mate's dad's house who gave up his season ticket a few years ago. He had the full-season Setanta package, so me and three mates invade his place, kick his dog out and his wife (sorry) every couple of weeks to watch the away matches. So round we all go and settle down with half a dozen bottles of beer each.

Now I have to be honest and say that throughout the ninety minutes a lot of the talk wasn't really about what was happening on the pitch at Easter Road. Much of the chat was about restructuring the team for the following season. Who's good enough, who's not, new manager etc. (particularly as Gordon Marshall had made a bit of a mess of things at Fir Park). "But look at the trophies he's won!" All the usual stuff.

It was around about the 75-minutes mark that an argument/disagreement finally erupted about what we were watching.

"This is boring as fuck, let's have a look to see if Motherwell are anywhere near an equaliser."

"No fucking way are those bastards going on ma telly."

Finally, after about 10 minutes of this he relented and over it went. I will never forget the next ten seconds as long as I live. He flipped the channel over, but being the technophobe he is, he got it wrong and Eurosport popped up.

"Aw come on, sort yourself out man," we joked.

He got it right this time and as we adjust to what we are seeing someone is having a feeble shot at goal (not sure yet which way the teams are shooting). A small guy in the box controls it on his chest, it sits up nicely. Bang. Goal. We start celebrating in turn, one after the other as it becomes apparent what is going on. Head in the hands type stuff. Disbelief. Then as the beggars kick off, it's every man for himself. Shouting all sorts of nonsense with no-one actually listening to anybody else. Complete panic / euphoria / shock, God knows what. I notice some additional bodies gathering in his kitchen. The wife has returned, and some inquisitive neighbours are sticking their heads round the door. A dog is in the living room. The sense of panic has transferred to it, I kid you not!

Arguments start again about which game we should be watching. We agree to get the Bears on. But hang on... here come Motherwell.

"Awwww where the fuck are you going son? Corner flag for fucks sake son! Oh, he's into the box. Cut back, cut back, don't shoot from... YYEEEEEESSSSSSSSS!"

Absolute bedlam.

Amid celebrations, I try to get the point across that we need to see the Bears game NOW! We flip the channel to watch the Rangers stroke the ball along the halfway line to clinch title number 51. A period of surreal calm then develops for me. Just sitting sipping beer, looking at the floor.

"Unbelievable. Unbelievable," keeps running through my head. Having gone through a similar hell of not being in control at Ibrox 2 years earlier I was convinced that was a once in a lifetime experience as far as supporting the Gers was concerned. Thankfully, I was wrong. Thank you Rangers, an amazing day.

Ross Gourlay

I remember waking up in the morning feeling terrible - I'd been out the night before and I clearly remember a bit of banter and putting on a bet with a Celtic supporting friend(ish) about us winning the league, although I honestly couldn't see it happening. A quick stop at the shops to get supplies and on the way down the road, another Tim mate starts honking his horn and shouting championees out his car window, only to get a friendly finger in return.

The car journey to Edinburgh was as grim as I'd ever had, falling asleep trying to get rid of this hangover. I woke up just as we were entering Edinburgh and I forced down a couple of tins to get in the mood. The Bears were in good voice and there was definitely a buzz around us. But halfway through the first half, when the Hibs fans started cheering and celebrating, I started to think this just wasn't gonna be our day. My stomach was still groaning. Half-time and I noticed Stuart McCall was only a few seats away. Onto the phone to my dad (he was sitting further along) and saying, "As long as it's one, you never know."

We got the goal, but at the time it was only half celebrated, knowing we've done our part but we still need to hear from the other end. Then came the roar! It swept from left to right along the stand and I knew why, but I didn't want to believe it! Surely a false alarm! People were shouting, hugging, celebrating all over the place but I just couldn't join in until I knew!

Then I received a text saying it was 1-1!

YES!

The euphoria died down and then the longest two minutes of my life ensued, just waiting to hear that they'd regained the lead. And then another roar!

Full-time!

It must be ours!

Then people shouting 2-1. The fear came back in, have Celtic managed to win it? I've never been so confused!

My mate text me telling me Scott McDonald had gotten a second for Motherwell! Then the fans ran on the pitch and the Gers players were celebrating - I knew it was ours!

The hangover seemed to vanish! I met my dad outside after the celebrations, he didn't even know it was 2-1!

"Ha, ha so we won the league on points as well! Get it up them!"

On the way back up the road there was a commotion in front - I thought it was a fight but, would you believe it, there's Big Marv hanging out his sunroof being mobbed from supporters! I managed to squeeze in and shake the big man's paw (and have the car run over my wee toe). Back to Forfar lads - time to celebrate!

Scott Blair

Don't have much of a story, as I was stuck offshore on an oil rig in the North Sea with the radio on. When Motherwell's first goal went in I, a normally quiet and shy guy, started screaming and basically going off my nut in sheer delight and had three or four Norwegian guys run into my office to find out what the hell was going on, as they thought I was being attacked.

I then met a few fellow Bears in the tea shack and we proceeded to do a huddle and have a wee sing-song in celebration of what we had just listened to. I had to wait three days before I could celebrate properly with a beer, but I sure made up for it when I did.

William Withers

Went to the Stumps pub just off Dumbarton Road with my parents and brother more in hope than expectation. When Celtic scored I clearly remember saying to my old man, "There's no way they will let that scoreline slip." Little did I know.

Coming near the end of the games, I was getting more and more depressed with the thought of their title celebrations and the coverage in the media over the next few days/weeks. With about 10 minutes to go the power goes out in the pub. Cue shouts of, "What the fuck is going on, anybody an electrician, who's got a tranny?"

To make matters even worse, the electronic tills wouldn't open and the staff weren't willing to sell more drink. Sitting in a dark boozer with no idea what was happening was doing our box in so we made our way out to head across the road to another pub only to hear a cheer from back inside. Barged back in to be told by a guy with his ear glued to the radio that Motherwell had scored. Turned to my brother and said, "He's making it up," as I simply couldn't believe what was happening. My second mistake of the day.

We stood staring at this guy and asking what was going on when the power suddenly came back on and we saw the

Bears doing the bouncy at Easter Road. The news then came through that Motherwell had scored a second. I've never had a feeling quite like that moment. We went berserk and stormed the bar. The second cheapest bottle of bubbly was well and truly dispatched, which led onto a night I'll never forget. Thank you Rangers.

Billy McKee

I was at the Old Firm game a few weeks earlier and was gutted to hear them celebrate like they had already won the league. I was so down I decided to book a week away in Spain. I was fairly cheered up that week then I got a text from my mate telling me that the Hibees had won at Parkhead. We still had a slim chance.

On Helicopter Sunday I was back at work in Dublin preparing for a night shift. I spent the morning in bed too nervous to listen to the game on the radio. I never slept, instead I dreamt of Motherwell scoring a late equaliser and even believe it or not, a late winner. I knew, though, that it was just a dream and that jammy lot would probably sneak it.

I decided to get out of bed with approx 10 mins remaining 'just in case'. I checked the Sky text and to my absolute horror it was as I'd expected. Rangers up 1-0 and Celtic also winning 1-0. My dream had gone in an instant and that sick feeling returned to the pit of my stomach. I turned over to Sky News and just at that precise moment they went for a sports update. The words of the anchor man froze me to the spot… "Rangers are just moments away from clinching the SPL title".

My heart raced and the phone went… "What the fuck was going on?" I answered the phone just as the anchor man said, "Motherwell have just scored again and the title is heading to Ibrox." The phone call was from my mum, she was screaming on the other end of the phone, "We've won the league!"

I was in a sleepy daze but that sick feeling had been replaced with a childlike excitement and a realisation that this was a special moment. I hung up the phone after speaking to my entire family, sat for a silent moment and wept.

The Rangers had done the impossible and it was the worst ever outcome for 'them'. What a combination. I proudly marched into work that night only to see loads of Irish lads piling out of work with the green and grey on. They had gone to work expectantly that morning, the parties had been arranged, the holiday for Monday booked, all was well in their world. But we fucked it up for them and I was a proud Bear in my Dublin office that night.

Alexander McGregor

Best day of my footballing life. Was in the pub in town and at half-time I was almost 99.99% sure it was over. Could not believe the cheek I would be facing and was hearing in the pub as the majority were unfortunately Timmies. We did have one Motherwell fan though, no joke, he's staunch as anything too.

Anyways, a weird celebration for Novo's goal which was laughed off by Tim. Then when the noise exploded from our fans and noises came from all around there was that nervous butterfly sensation in me and other Bluenoses.

When we heard for sure Motherwell had scored it was the best feeling I think I've ever had. Table was knocked over, drinks went everywhere, even the barman was going mental.

After that the second goal killed us as we just lost the

plot and hugged randoms and laughed at Timmy before jumping up and down outside like madmen.

The best day in history, it won't be closer than that ever again.

Rangers I LOVE YOU!

Dougie McIntosh

Not having Setanta, my brother and I went round to a mate's house to watch the game. Just me, my bro, my mate and his sister. Time ticked by and nothing was happening - we were all talking about how these idiots will take over the town that night and ruin another night out. Sutton scores and there is serious depression all round. Never wanted to throw something at a TV so much in my whole life.

Still, there was plenty of 'gallows humour' about - still laugh at some of the chances they missed that day… could see it on their faces - the look of 'so what - we will still win this'. It seems that the whole day just started to speed up from the time Nacho scored - the only other thing I remember happening was Agathe clearing the ball off the line with his face and falling down as if he had been hit by a truck (something we were almost on the floor laughing at). Then it happened… the strangest 5 seconds of our lives. Chick Young screams on the radio, "Rangers will be the SPL champions!"

We were sitting with the TV turned down (Celtic game on) and the Gers game on the radio. Cue four people staring at each other for about 2 or 3 seconds… then turning to look at the TV as my brother says, "What is that prick talking abo…"

Scott McDonald. One swing of that boot and the four of us almost lost control of our bodily functions. When I think back, I can still feel the rasp on the back of my throat from the scream I gave when that goal went in. It's an overused phrase... but a true 'classic'. Then it hit you - there was still time.

Gers were safe - Hibs helped by not pushing forward... they had what they wanted.

Celtic were the experts at last minute goals. This time though, there was a difference. Celtic looked like a broken team. We sat, shaking, not knowing whether to laugh, cry, sing, jump... I couldn't sit down... just too nervous. Then it happened... Chick Young again on the Radio... for a moment we thought they had scored... then we heard it was Motherwell again. This time we did celebrate. My mate ran about screaming - the rest of us just jumping about the living room like idiots. Then out the back of the house to get drenched in champagne... well, I did anyway.

Then it was over to Ibrox for the party. Will it ever be repeated? I hope not, it's a memory that is tucked away up there to be brought out whenever things seem to be not as bright - or if you ever, ever have to remind yourself of what it means to be a Rangers fan. One of The People. Legend.

Archie Gemmell

I was in the house myself that day preparing the evening meal. I had the radio on listening to the game. Rangers were obviously winning when the wife came home. She started nattering away and was beginning to catch my attention when I heard the goal come in from Fir Park. I let out a roar and turned the radio up. The wife went upstairs in the huff. Then I heard Motherwell's second goal go in and started dancing about the house.

I opened the back door and heard another Bear, some distance away, over the top of my back garden, shouting, "Ya fucking beauty!" If you've ever seen that episode of Rab

C Nesbitt where he meets his Spanish doppelganger, that was EXACTLY the scenario I was involved in. Never found out yet who that Bear was.

The dinner went on at a peep and I went to the Club to await the arrival of the brethren who'd attended the game at Easter Road. One of the best nights I've EVER had in that Club.

I got wrecked.

The dinner got burnt.

The wife fell out with me and I fell down the stairs at home wrecking my back and losing weeks off work. I just wish I could do it all over again!

Craig Abernethy

Well, as every Gers fan will say, 22nd May 2005 is unbeatable in football terms. It seems so long ago, but will always be with us till the day we die.

My friends Colin, Tambo, Stevie and me (Craig) set off to Stevie's house in Paisley for a few drinks before the match. We then headed round to Simons Bar in Renfrew, this was the first time any of us had been there. We were talking about the ifs and buts like everyone else would have been and praying inside that it could happen! Even the famous old line 'KEEP BELIEVING'.

When the game started the pub was quiet as expected, then when wee Nacho missed the sitter you thought, it's gonna be one of those days. Can't remember much more of the first half, apart from Mutton scoring for them.

When the wee man scored, the place erupted and you could feel the confidence grow in the place.

Again, the rest of the second half from our game is a sheer blur!

In Simons there was a lounge next door with the Celtic

My Helicopter Sunday

game on and you could gauge what was happening through the game. Then it happened, the roar from next door.

The place was jumping, I even accidentally smashed a glass frame on the wall with my elbow (sorry about that, whoever the owner was. I offered him £20 after the game, but he wouldn't take it). When we saw the goal filtered through on the Gers game it was even better.

There was an awkward couple of minutes watching us pass about the ball at the back, everyone asking frantically in confusion why Hibs weren't attacking us. Trying to listen in to their game. I was shaking, don't know if it was fear of them scoring, excitement, or a bit of both.

Then another cheer and the place went mental. Maybe the best feeling in the world, that's the only way you can describe it. To realize we had just won the league in the last minutes of the season against our greatest, or should I say worst, rivals!

After the game we had planned to go to see my brother's friend, David, who had broken his ankle the day before (playing footy after he was pished watching the FA Cup Final - the break was a bad one by the way!) Suffice to say that was blown out the window.

We decide to go to the Brox to see the team with the trophy. We went far too early, we were in the front of the Copland. We started to sober up in the heat but it didn't matter as we were drunk on adrenaline. The party mood was amazing. The sun was out and the songs on the PA, *Amarillo* and *Come on over to my place*, were fantastic. Such a great day!

When the players came running out with the trophy it was something to behold.

Then after about 10 minutes the neds started running on (what did they expect to happen, the players just to be flooded with fans?). That was the only downer on the day, but at least we saw the players and manager with the trophy for 10 minutes.

We then went to a neutral pub in Paisley. It had a few of 'them' still in drowning their sorrows and that only added to a great day.

After a good few drinks we decided to go and get something to eat. We were heading to an Indian restaurant when this wee idiot started shouting from across the street. What he never realized was our pal Tam had stopped to tie his laces just behind him. We shouted

over, "Tam, boot his baws," and the wee guy hasn't run so fast in his life I bet!

After the meal as we were heading back to Stevie's (for more drink) this fox was at the side of the street. We gave it a full nan bread, the greedy bastard, then we started singing, "If you hate Neil Lennon swoosh your tail!" We still sing that to this day, thinking back to that night!

Well that rounds off the craziest, most unexpected day in my 26 years!

"Things that are impossible with men, are possible with God." Keep Believing!

Just one more thing:

Scott McDonald scored two goals, E I E I O!

With an overhead kick and a cheeky wee flick, He made those fuckin' bastards sick.

Scott McDonald scored two goals, E I E I O!

Jim Rennie

The Gers were playing the Hibs at Easter Road and I was running late so I was standing at the corner looking for

My Helicopter Sunday

a taxi to get me to supporters' bus on time. Wife was standing at front window of flat looking along main road and spots taxi coming. Opens window to shout to me when window cord snaps and slams down sending glass showering down to street. That's it, I thought, no game for me, need to go back up and board up window. Then Timmy neighbour shouts down, "Away and see yer team win the league, youse have waited long enough. I'll board yer windae up."

So off I go to see Colin Stein score and big ham and eggs getting our hands on the Trophy and stop Timmy doing 10 in a row.

Following week ordered new double-glazed windows.

Fast forward 30 years (and I am living elsewhere) and I am on supporters' bus on my way to Easter Road again with the Gers having the slimmest of chances of winning the league. But I am telling (with tongue in cheek) anybody who will listen that we will win it.

Why?

Because as before I had had a mishap with a window the week before and had placed an order to have new double glazing installed. I had also taken with me a digital camera I had recently bought and wanted to try it out.

Come that memorable moment when news was filtering through from Motherwell that the Tims had bottled it and we were going to get our hands on the trophy I switched the camera to video mode and recorded the Bears round about me going mental. Came home and viewed the clip on computer and thought of all those Bears at home and around the world who had not sampled the euphoria that I had experience that day. So put the clip on Putfile and posted a link on *Follow Follow*.

Immediately I was bombarded with PMs with request

for copies, so over the next 24/48 hours my fingers were aching sending them to all parts of the world. America, Australia, Middle East, Europe, Far East they were sent until a kindly Bear hosted it on his website.

Then came a request from Rangers TV asking if they could use it on a programme they were doing about Helicopter Sunday which they duly broadcast with my name on the end credits. I believe that between Putfile and YouTube it has been viewed over 100,000 times.

Never was I so proud to be a Bluenose than I was that week and I still get goose-bumps when I think of that glorious day in our history.

Martin Grier

Friday afternoon and work's finished for the week so we're heading into town for a few beers. The guy I'm with is a Dundee fan and he asks if I think the Gers can do it. Can we do it? I want to say yes but that lot are so fuckin' jammy you just know that no matter what way the scores go they'll steal it right at the death.

After a few beers I leave the pub with my mate's parting words, "Good luck on Sunday mate."

I return his words much the same way, I think Dundee had a relegation battle that weekend, but all I can think about as I walk out is, it's the start of the weekend but it's not long to Monday and those fuckin' gloating Tims!

Sunday comes and the usual pub we watch the Gers games in is showing the other match because 'It's the one everyone wants to see'.

Well we don't so it's off on a mad dash to find a boozer for Bears. A mate texts to say Ferrari's is showing the Teddy Bears so off we go and with a pint in my hand and the radio in my ear I'm all set.

It's 1-0 to both teams and deep down I'm wishing I'd stayed at home. The old man says, "How's it going, still the same?"

The answer is a disappointed, "Yes."

But then something happens and you know how it is on the radio. You think you're 1-0 up then find out your team missed and someone's went up the other end and scored. This was different. I'm thinking, McDonald - who the fuck does he play for? Then I realize, "Yeeeeeesssssss! 1-1, 1-1, 1-1!"

We're jumping about like maniacs but then it's, "How long left?" or "Those jammy bastards will still get another."

Just then the commentator starts getting excited, it's this guy McDonald again, and it's 2-1!

"2-1! 2-1 CHAMPIONEEEES!"

Now the goals are playing in the bottom of the screen and everyone is going fuckin' crazy, jumping on each other. A major piss-up is on the cards now. We're all singing and people are coming down from a private function upstairs to check the scores. It wasn't hard to spot the Tims.

A workmate on holiday texts me asking for the scores, he's in the airport waiting to come home after 2 weeks in the sun. I text back, Rangers 1 Hibs 0, Celtic 1 Motherwell... (with enough spaces to keep him guessing)... 2 CHAMPIONS AGAIN 51 LEAGUE TITLES!!!!

He didn't believe me, so a long distance call to mummy was made to confirm the news. In his case it was bad news 'cos he's a Tim. HA! HA! HA!

Monday arrived and with a bit of a hangover lingering in my head I make my way to work. I know I won't be able to keep the smile off my face when I see them and when I do I just say, "I've got this morning's papers if you want a read."

I get a mumble of some sort which I take as a 'NO' which is good. I didn't spend all that money on papers to let some Tim get a free read. I don't think the guy in the shop had sold so many papers to one person.

Even after all this time we still smile at that day and for a country with its so called 'secret shame' someone with more faith than most told us to, "Keep believing," and someone else looked down as if to say, "You don't have to believe anymore, it has happened."

We really are the people, keep the faith.

Barry Mathieson

Taxi is waiting outside to take me and my mates to Glasgow city centre for the game. I look at the case of champagne (don't ask) sitting in my kitchen and ponder whether to put it in the fridge or not. Decide not to bother as not too optimistic despite big Marvin's pleas! Arrive at the Hall on Sauchiehall Street just a little after kick off. They are showing the Bears game while next door O'Neill's has the other game.

A bit subdued but decide to make the most of it as there are about 12 of us including my sister and girlfriend. They go one up and nobody is surprised but nobody cheers which is a bonus as the pub is heaving.

Wee Nacho scores to perk us up a bit. Then it happens, the one guy in the pub with a radio stands up and shouts, "Motherwell have scored!" but we don't accept this till Setanta show the goal in the corner of the screen. The blood drains from my face and I actually feel sick. My girlfriend says I turned a shade of green (irony?) and I had to go outside for air. Then it happens again!

While outside trying not to faint I see a guy watching

the Sellick game through O'Neill's window then he jumps up and down screaming then runs down towards me.

"Is it finished? Is it finished?"

"No Motherwell have scored again!"

WWWOOOOWWW OH MY GOD.

I don't feel faint or sick anymore as I know we have done it. I run like a madman back into the pub, jump on top of my mates and gradually the words come out, "We have bloody done it, they are getting beat!" Then about 10 seconds later the goal comes up on screen. Time for the bouncy we think. Sight of the day was O'Neill's emptying two minutes later and passing the big glass windows watching us bounce.

You don't need to guess that we ended up back at mine emptying a box of champagne into the freezer although most got sprayed over the streets of Knightswood that night. One of my mates from that day got married a couple of weeks ago and in his speech he said that his wedding day was the happiest day of his life except of course for Helicopter Sunday. Says it all probably.

Thank you Rangers (till I die).

bluenose baz

Spent the first half in the house listening on the radio. My mate, a Celtic fan, was in a mixed pub down our way and kept asking me to go down. At half-time, with the league heading to Parkhead, I said to the missus I'm off to the pub, I'd rather see us losing it than listen on the radio.

When I got to the pub I asked my mate if he wanted a drink, bottle of champagne was his reply. I laughed and bought the cheeky runt a pint.

There were 2 TVs in the pub, one with our game, and one with their game. After Rangers scored, every person in the pub was watching the Celtic game.

We all know what happened, I've never been so happy in my life. I bought my mate his champagne and partied all night. We hung a massive union flag outside the pub as the Celtic fans had to drive by on their way back from Fir Park. I now have 'keep believing 22/05/05' tattooed on my arm.

David Stewart

I remember sitting in the house on the Saturday night, texting a girl from the supporters' bus who was also going the next day, and I said to her, "We will win the league tomorrow." To be honest I didn't really believe it, it was just a sort of last act of defiance. Got up the next morning early as, fuck, couldn't sleep. For some reason I had a 'feeling' about that day. Couldn't put my finger on it but just in the back of my mind there was this nagging feeling that we were gonna do it.

Another mate sent a text to me. It was unbelievable, about three pages long, a massive rallying call saying we were the people, no surrender etc. Anyways, goes over to Edinburgh and into a boozer where there's a group of guys sitting singing, "We're gonna win the league." People were laughing, but this just added to the feeling that I had.

On to the game. Remember getting a taxi up Easter Road and as we got out a Hibs fan walked by singing, "You're gonna win feck all."

"Just what you always win," came the reply from my mate.

Remember Sutton scoring, then I just sort of felt resigned to the fact we were gonnae lose it. Even when Novo scored, I didn't really celebrate as much as the other Bears there.

Then into the last five minutes, you could feel an eerie

silence had descended on the place. Everyone was pretty depressed and feeling resigned to the inevitable. I remember looking at my watch, quarter to fourish, and thinking it's now or never. Then about ten seconds later, it happened. The biggest explosion of emotion I have ever seen at a football match. Everyone was going absolute nuts.

After it had calmed down I was standing, close to tears, shaking like feck, thinking either Celtic or Hibs would score. Then it happened again, another roar. At first I thought the Celtic game was full-time, and all I remember is my mate from the bus shouting, "It's 2-1, it's 2-1," before giving me a big kiss

After the game our bus went to Ibrox to see the team returning, then we went to the District where the team came down later. Wee Nacho and Bob Malcolm were up on the bar singing and dancing. Magic!

Lawson Barrie

It shames me to say I never attended Easter Road on this most historic of days, nor did I even watch the action unfold on TV. I didn't buy into the whole 'Keep believing' line of thought and had more or less conceded that another title had been lost to our greatest rivals. Instead I was playing golf in Ayrshire (can't remember where exactly) and knew nothing about the scores of the two games until just after half-time.

Got back to the clubhouse and my fears seemed justified. Celtic 1-0 up and cruising (or so I thought) to the title, while we were locked at 0-0 with Hibs. Listened to the last 40 minutes or so of the Motherwell game on the radio (the clubhouse didn't have Setanta), feeling numb at the thought of ending the season with just the CIS cup to show for our efforts. Then, a ray of hope in the form of top scorer Nacho Novo who had edged us ahead at Easter Road.

I remember someone shouting, "It must have hit his backside," as the goal was announced, referring to the fact that Novo's form had dipped dramatically towards the end of the season. It was ironic that the Spaniard was the scorer, such had been his bad luck in front of goal in the few weeks previous.

My next memory is McDonald scoring to make it 1-1 and me jumping for joy and hugging anyone and everyone in sight! What a feeling, maybe the best moment of my life, and I mean that sincerely.

The pessimist in me meant that my next thought was, Celtic have a knack of scoring late goals. Thankfully this was not realised and 'Skippy' added another and the rest is history. The relief at the final whistle was incomparable, we had achieved the unthinkable. I met up with a fellow season ticket holder and we duly headed to Ibrox for the party. The somewhat sarcastic, "Easy, easy!" chants are my abiding memory, as our 51st title had been anything but easy. But I wouldn't have had it any other way. What a day, what a conclusion, never to be forgotten. Needless to say, I am now a believer!

Andy Cumming

Remember the day well, a sunny Sunday in May.

I got up and thought to myself, I hope I get a ticket, as I had been to every game that season (I think) but hadn't got hold of a ticket for this match at Easter Road. A game that I thought would be an end-of-season affair and we had little chance of winning the title. I made my way down to where our bus meets and was told there was a ticket for me. That was a good start to the day but never in my wildest dreams did I realise what was to follow!

We made our way to Easter Road and many of us went to the Masonic in Leith for a pre-match refreshment and I bumped into many well known faces. Also ex-Ger Stuart McCall was there and that made a lot of people happy as he was only to pleased to sign autographs and get pictures taken with fans. It was approaching kick off so we started making our way to the ground and, funnily enough, Stuart McCall came in and sat beside me. Pure coincidence, but I told him he must have been following me!

Not long into the game the Hibs fans cheered and those amongst our support with radios confirmed that Celtic had scored. That was that in most people's minds but fair play to the Bears who stayed to a man and supported their team with pride. Rangers eventually scored a well worked goal credited to Novo but I'm sure Celtic player Gary Caldwell got the final touch!

Hibs and Rangers then played out the game which, other than a Novo miss earlier, wasn't up to much to be honest. But the manner in which the game was won was not important to anyone! With a couple of minutes to go many Bears let out a cheer and news filtered through that Motherwell had scored. Many people did not believe it. More people started getting texts and calls confirming this and the place started going nuts. Then came more news of another goal at Motherwell and most thought that Celtic, who often get late winners, may have done it again. But no, that man Scott McDonald had doubled Well's lead and the bedlam began. The final whistle had gone in Edinburgh and we just awaited news that the game was over in Lanarkshire. It soon was and the feeling will stay with me for ever. It was unbelievable, a combination of absolute joy, mild shock and a good few emotions chucked in the mix too! I remember a pitch invasion of sorts that was good natured and that was cleared and the party continued. We just awaited the trophy to arrive and it soon did. What a feeling.

We made our way back to our bus after the presentation and after a good few more victory songs inside the stadium. To be honest, the bus was great for a while then went quiet, guys could not believe the day that they had just witnessed and been part of! We got back to Paisley and got off the bus where we did a huddle in the middle of the street, and this soon turned in to a bouncy! We went in to the pub and met mates who were equally as happy. Many said they saw me and others on the TV. One of the lads decided he'd have a party in the house so we wandered up to his but many of us drifted away quite early. I got home around 10:30pm and began to reflect on the day's events!

The day we won the league at Easter Road (Wolverhampton Town Tune) by Andy Cumming

It was one Sunday in May, when the Gers were due to play
To win the league our chances they were low,
To Edinburgh we'd go hoping for a show,
When Rangers won the league at Easter Road.

(Chorus) There's not a team like the Glasgow Rangers,
One of the famous songs we sung.
There were cheers and songs and laughter
We'll remember ever after
When the Rangers won the league at Easter Road.
Not long left to go and the Celts they were one up
The title it was heading Celtic's way.
Then the Bears at Easter Road heard Motherwell had scored,

And there's still ninety seconds left to play.
The fans could not believe it, just what was going on?
To Bears were so delighted it was true.
Then came in the news, that Well had scored again.
We'd won the league again, now we were sure.

Chorus

The trophy it was bound for Motherwell they said.
It was in a helicopter that they flew.
It had to change direction to Edinburgh it went
So it could be decked out red, white and blue.
The Bears at Easter Road were singing all their songs
An atmosphere that will be hard to beat.
The Gers were so elated, the Celts they were deflated.
The way the league was won was oh so sweet.

Chorus

There was Barry, Dado, Buffel, Rae and Nacho Novo
Big Marv, Soti and Arveladze too,
Big Ronald and Fernando and Stefan Klos was there
With all the other heroes dressed in blue.
That crazy day in May, it was the twenty-second
It is an afternoon we'll all remember
And we sang *Sunshine on Leith* to the Hibees disbelief.
The day we won the league at Easter Road.
There's not a team like the Glasgow Rangers
One of the famous songs we sung
There were cheers and songs and laughter
We'll remember ever after
When Rangers won the league at Easter Road,

When Rangers won the league at Easter Road.

David McCorquodale/David Fleming

Me and my mate never had a ticket for Helicopter Sunday but a guy on *Follow Follow* called huggybear said his brother won 2 tickets in a Daily Record competition but he couldn't go. So my mate sent him a PM. My mate was first to reply and we met him through the week, gave him the cash and we went to Easter Road front door and collected the two tickets. We couldn't believe our luck getting into this match and the rest is history.

George Wilson

I was resigned to the fact that they would win the league and set about my day as per a normal Sunday. My oldest son was playing football for his under-13 boys' club team and on the way back he commented that, "They seem to be everywhere today Dad," after passing several carry-out-laden green and grey clad horrors obviously heading to celebratory parties.

"Let them have their day," says super-sensible *moi*. Until wee Nacho scored.

We turned the channel over to watch the Celtic game after the goal 'cos it didn't matter what happened in our game. I'll never forget the joy that erupted in my house when McDonald scored. I slid along the floor and ended up in tears whilst cuddling my boys and nephew. And I repeated this at the second goal and full-time.

I managed to phone a couple of babysitters and made it to my local boozer which was jumping by then. I've never seen so many grown men cuddling each other. The good lady was there as well and just shook her head and laughed when she saw me (I think she was more than expecting me).

I managed to make it to work for a 7am start the next day, despite being rough as a badger's, much to the surprise of a few of my workmates.

Andrew Johnston

Bizarrely, my story begins in the toilet of the Clachan on Paisley Road West 'cos that's where I bought my ticket for the game!

I'm the first to admit I didn't fully believe. It was more blind hope that made me buy it and a chance to show them even if we don't win it we will still go and sing louder and longer than anyone else!

After the journey from Dumfries, a few drinks, a really bad fake for £5 for one of the boys and a ten minute wait outside the stand I got in to join a lung-bursting *No Surrender* and watch Hibs flash one across goal!

Nacho's goal was celebrated more than usual of course and started a spark of belief in me and about 4000 others!

Got a few texts at about 85 minutes saying I had been on the telly. Cue the thoughts of, Jesus I hope I wasn't doing something stupid.

And then it can only be described as all hell breaking loose! The guy beside me had a radio and he just went mental and so did everybody else. The next two minutes was mayhem and is still a blur in my mind!

After more mayhem which I thought was the final whistle at Fir Park, it was simply amazing! Everyone there began to realise what we were witnessing and it was one hell of a party. It still seems surreal to this day and it all went so fast!

The Rangers fans on the pitch, then the Hibs players,

the Hibs fans, the police horses, the Rangers players and then the SPL trophy!

The party went on outside, meeting mates from the top tier, mass bouncies going down Easter Road, and constant, "You're never gonna believe us…"

I phoned a mate who was in Vegas to spread the word, telling him they drew 1-1 only to be told by a passer-by it was 2-1!

First tune on the bus was The Drifters *Come on over to my place*. Every song in the book was sung over and over all the way home followed by a 'few' drinks and telling the story of it over and over again! What a first day of my week's holiday! Carlsberg don't do Sundays…

Ian Cathcart

This day will ALWAYS go down as the best day in my life. Went through to Edinburgh early so we could get in the boozer at 12:30 opening time. It was my dad's turn to drive. Had an enjoyable hour scooping a few ales and telling my dad/cousin/pal that we were going to do it. I was convinced.

Phoned Ladbrokes for a price on the way to the game and ended up not taking it.

I remember crying with happiness once it had all sunk in.

I remember singing *Sunshine on Leith* at the top of my voice.

I remember cuddling anyone in the ground near me.

I remember the team sprinting out of the tunnel.

I remember the police horses on the park.

I remember the astonishment on everyone's face.

I remember getting about 20 texts from mates saying, 'Just seen you doing the easy clap on the TV'.

I remember Ricksen in front of the team lifting the cup.

I remember Hibs fans trying to get on the park from the Main Stand for a fight.

I remember the walk up Easter Road, place going mental.

I remember Big Marv out the sunroof of a car on Easter Road, hands raised like the Messiah.

I remember stopping for a carry-out.

I remember driving through Princes Street and Corstorphine Road and getting stuck in the traffic when the French rugby fans were coming out of Murrayfield after the European Cup Final.

I remember getting back to Ibrox and getting parked on Edmiston Drive.

I remember the team bus arriving back minutes after us and dancing all over Edmiston Drive in front of it.

I remember getting in to the Broomloan rear (with what was left of our carry-out).

I WILL ALWAYS REMEMBER.

Craig Onslow

Venue: Cheers Bar, Port Harcourt, Nigeria.
Date: 22nd May 2005

The day started normal enough. Well, as normal as working in Nigeria could be!

I was living in an apartment directly across from Cheers Bar and went to the pub for my usual Sunday breakfast. I was hoping to catch some sort of coverage or updates on the games, at worst. To be honest, I wasn't overly excited as I was convinced the day was going to end in disappointment.

Now, I should say here that every year a Celtic-supporting friend of mine and I always have a bet on who will win the SPL. Danny lives in Liverpool but at the time was working in Paris. There are quite a few of us contractors (mercenaries) on the oil and gas circuit who travel around wherever the work or money is. Two weeks prior to 22nd May, Danny had great delight in sending an e-mail to me in Nigeria (and copying it to a hundred others all over the world) with his address for posting off his 20 Euros winnings for that season. The usual wind-up which was to come back and bite him in the arse!

Anyway, I had a word with the bar manager in Cheers but it quickly became apparent that there was no chance of catching any updates, due to cricket and motor racing being the sports of choice for the pub's majority.

I had spoken to my wife earlier that day and assured her that all was well. A daily phone call was the norm due to the kidnappings in the Niger Delta area. She asked if I would see the game and I told her that since I was in the minority there was no hope of watching it, or even keeping updated with the scores.

I quickly got down to a few games of pool with my mate, a Millwall fan, while all the time trying to forget that as we played, Rangers were fighting it out at Easter Road in the hope that Celtic would slip up at Fir Park. I actually started winning a few games and then we were joined by some Nigerians who wanted to play. We got into some betting with them over a few games and the pool table area started getting quite boisterous due to the large sums of money changing hands. Some of the lads from the lounge area actually started coming through to see what all the commotion was.

Then to my surprise my mobile started ringing. Who could that be? The number said it was my wife. As we only ever spoke to each other once a day I thought, what does she want now? I stopped playing pool and answered the phone. Couldn't hear a word she said due the large crowd around the pool table. "Sssshhhhh!", I shouted, "I'm on the phone here!"

Wife: "Rangers have won the league."

<pause>

Wife: "Hello?"

Me: "What do you want?"

Wife: "What do you mean?"

Me: "Look, I'm in the middle of a game of pool here, are you taking the piss or what?"

Wife: "No, I'm serious. They beat Hibs 1-0 and Motherwell have beaten Celtic 2-1!"

Well, I was speechless, I didn't know what to say. Everyone was looking at me thinking something was wrong.

Me: "RANGERS HAVE WON THE LEAGUE!"

That moment was the starting point of a night of celebrations, probably which will never be matched again. I had all the pool room cheering, all the locals were slapping me on the back and so on. I was in a state of shock. I couldn't wait to get to work on the Monday to answer Danny's e-mail.

God only knows what **he** must have been thinking. To this day, I don't think he has overcome the embarrassment of that e-mail he sent (or my reply 2 weeks later). One thing though, I didn't receive an e-mail the following season even when we were so far behind Celtic that there was more chance of Hell freezing over than us catching them!

Gary Hamilton

Never being an optimistic fellow, I should have been approaching the last Sunday of the season like a 'glass half empty'. But some mischievous sprite kept telling me to go to the pub, you never know what might happen. That mischievous sprite wasn't some figment of my imagination or any second sight, it was my wee friend Ronnie the Half Pint. I met him in that well known haunt of West End Rangers supporters, the Stirling Castle.

Before getting to the pub I had to fight off approaches from my wife who was insisting I go with her on a sponsored walk around Strathclyde Park. Fortunately she realised that there were strange ions in the air that day and nothing would keep me from the pub so she dropped me off and wished me luck. Although she did say as I got out the car, "Don't build your hopes up too much."

I won't dwell on our goal or most of our match but I will dwell upon one guy who took a call on his mobile and stood up on a table saying, "Whit?"

The whole pub hushed and looked towards this guy as if everyone understood why he was standing on a table to take a phone call. The pub was silent except for the noise of our support on the telly as the news filtered through to them. As the support at Easter Road started to celebrate, our tabletop friend looked up and said the three words I'd been hoping to hear all day, "Motherwell have scored."

Bedlam ensued; I've never seen so much lager hanging in the air as every arm went up and the pub let out a roar which alerted my friend Murray who was at the petrol station down the street, filling his car after travelling back from a wedding in a huff at missing the game - he heard the roar and was in the Stirling Castle in a twinkling, bouncing with the best of them.

I'm sure we were still celebrating when back onto the table appears our astonishing fellow with the mobile clamped tight against his ear. This time he jumped, "They've scored again!"

Whoever had bought another pint upon losing the first one after the first goal, lost that one too and again it rained lager onto men and women crammed so tight that the only movement to be made was to jump up and down on the spot with arms in the air. I was hugging wee Ronnie and Murray and some strangers from the bar and we were almost crying, "I can't believe it, I can't believe it."

Outside, my wife drew up in the car, got out and approached the doors. She could hear the noise inside and was wondering what was going on when a wee old man in a bunnet came dancing out onto the street. "We did it hen, Rangers huv won the league!"

She knew then that the car was going to end up dumped and that we weren't going home.

Gordon Clark

Never got a ticket for the match and pretty much never really did 'believe' we could do it on that final day. It was a strange afternoon. On one hand, I was looking forward to watching the game, on the other, not looking forward to the usual sick feeling you get when the Yahoos win the title.

I sat and watched the game on my own - the wife was lying sleeping on the couch and I was quietly engrossed sipping a beer and not getting too excited. When we scored to make it one nil that was me. I then started flicking it over to see how their game was going. I could see that as the time was going on, the Celtic players were beginning to make a few mistakes – stray passes and botched clearances from defence.

I saw Petrov shouting at his own players - basically beginning to show signs of nerves. I knew that something could be on here. I couldn't even have told you how close to full-time it was when Motherwell equalised. All I remember was the ball hitting the back of the net and I jumped up out of my seat throwing my arms up into the air and my right hand crashing against the Artex. I roared, "Ya feckin' beauty," and my wife got the fright of her life - almost ending up on the floor. She hadn't a clue what had happened. It was her that noticed that I had cut my hand on the Artex - I never even noticed.

I quickly flicked it over to our game just as the news got to the Bears and the place erupted. The players just stopped playing just looking around - they didn't know what to do.

I then flicked it back to the Motherwell game and my neighbour just came right in to our house, not even bothering to knock. He knew by my roars that Motherwell had scored. Just at that, the second goal went in and we were the champs. I had to go out the back to try to get some fresh air. I honestly thought I was going to pass out.

We went into town that night and what a sight it was, passing the Celtic pubs seeing them all just sitting on the pavement outside wondering where it all went wrong. The Bears in their cars were peeping their horns going past with the scarves and flags being waved out of the windows. A day I will never forget, but also wished I had taken the trip through to Ibrox to see the players.

Andrew

22nd May 2005 will go to my grave with me. Perhaps the greatest day I have ever had in all the years I have attended Rangers games. Perhaps it will be surpassed when/if we win the Champions League in the same manner Man United did against Bayern in 1999.

I took the car through, two mates and two girls from our RSC; it was more out of blind, bloody loyalty and the fact that we had nothing else to do that day. My mate Alan always said we would do it but he was dismissed. The defeat to Celtic at Ibrox seemed to have killed us off, but then the Green and Grey lost to Hibs. I think we won 1-0 at Dunfermline thanks to big Dado, and our last home game to set up the league decider for the 22nd May.

The calm before the……

Ya beauty!!!

My Helicopter Sunday

Sunshine on Leith

Howard arrives with the trophy. My old mate Alasdair
(second on left) welcomes him

Ian Stewart

Doc McGuiness in foreground changed days from The Ropework, eh Doc?

Preparing to deliver trophy to Fernando

My Helicopter Sunday

Yes! First is everything

We are the champions my friend!

Alex Rae remains calm in the chaos

It was worth coming home eh Barry?

My Helicopter Sunday

A Shola hug and more mad dancing

There's only one Nacho Novo

Marvellous Marvin pays homeage to his Congregation

The magnificent Dado Prso Men drink Milk!

My Helicopter Sunday

I was right guys 'keep believing'

Come on over to our place hey ya we're having a party

The game kicks off and we are straight on the attack. I think Alex Rae sent Novo clean through, the ball bounced over the keeper and Novo hit the post from a tight angle.

As far as football games go it was by no means a classic, but we had to win regardless of the performance. The girl who came through with us in the car had her radio on and told us Celtic were one up. We didn't, well I didn't, and neither did my mate Brian, expect anything else.

Buffel breaks forward, slots in Novo who in turn scores. Bedlam. I was sitting, well standing, in Row A in the Lower section of the stand. We came and got what we needed. We had to defend it or push on. Suddenly with perhaps 3 or 4 minutes left in our game, Tracy (the girl from the RSC) calm as you like turned to Brian and me, "1-1 with Celtic!"

Up it went. We are hugging each other, jumping around as if we had won the Euro millions. Novo looked across at the stand and I'm signalling '1-1' with my fingers. I don't know if he noticed me, but I'm certain it didn't take long for him or the rest of the players to figure out what was going on.

Unbelievable, it truly was unbelievable. I didn't know what to do, and we kept asking Tracy what else was going on. "Still 1-1." Next minute my mobile phone goes off, it's my auld man. I remember this like it was yesterday and looking at it on DVD I can see how people thought that the Celtic game finished 1-1. The conversation with my dad was these exact words:

Dad: "They are all over them."
Me, struggling to hear with all the noise: "Who?"
Dad: "Motherwell. They are all over them."
Me: "What's happening?"
Dad: "Wait… hang on…" silence… "2-1!"
I almost evacuated my bowels at the thought of Celtic

pulling it back.
Me: "Who to?"
Dad: "Motherwell."

I turned so quick to tell everyone that I felt a click in my back and I collapsed to my knees, struggling to breathe and trying to scream, "2-1 Motherwell!" I signalled to Brian that it was 2-1, and being the mate that he is, he didn't care to ask what was wrong with me, he simply grabbed me and said, "Who to?"

Bastard! As I picked myself up off the ground I am signalling '2-1' with my fingers to my fellow Bears in the stands. Some of their faces dropped thinking that Celtic had pulled off the escape.

Here is where people got a bit confused. Full-time sounded at Easter Road perhaps 5 to 10 seconds **after** Motherwell made it 2-1. So the 2nd roar (Motherwell's 2nd goal) was followed very quickly by the full-time whistle at Easter Road. If you look at Alex McLeish on the DVD when the 2nd roar went up Big Eck thought the game at Fir Park was over, but it was in fact Motherwell scoring their second. The full-time whistle then followed it at Easter Road.

Whilst we are singing and dancing in the stands the Celtic game is still taking place. Some Rangers fans had thought the Celtic game had finished 1-1 and some didn't even find out until the following day what the actual score was!

We headed back to the Empire Bar in Bannockburn for a glass of Irn Bru, but got stopped by the rugby fans leaving some Cup Final at Murrayfield. We have the songs blaring out the car and people were stopping to ask us what happened.

"Champions mate, Rangers are the Champions."

They didn't seem as pleased as we were! After much hugging and backslapping we got back to the pub and the rest is, well, a haze.

I went off travelling in Scandinavia with a sore back and met my future wife. Upon my return I had to consult an osteopath to check on my sore back. It appears when I turned quickly to let everyone know that Motherwell had taken the lead I had dislodged 6 joints in my back. After 18, £25 sessions to fix the problem I was right as rain again. I hear you ask at the back, "Was it worth it?" Bloody right it was and I would do it all over again for the rest of my life. The days like that don't come along often and certainly Hollywood couldn't have written a script for it.

Craig Watson

My Helicopter Sunday story actually starts on the 6th October 2004. That day, my dad fell seriously ill and went into hospital, 4 days later on the 10th of October my wee boy James was born. Then a couple of days later we were told my dad had terminal cancer and wasn't expected to survive very long. My dad Sandy Watson was born on the 22nd May 1954 and started taking me to games in early 1980 when I was 5. I went regularly until I had to stop going in 1994 due to work commitments. I started going back to the games regularly in 2000 and have been a regular since.

On the 26th of February 2005 my dad died. The night before his funeral we played Hearts at Tynecastle. I didn't want to go but was persuaded by both my wife and mum that it would do me good to get rid of some frustration. And with what happened in the last couple of minutes they couldn't have been more right.

Soto Kyrgiakos was pushed in the box, Dado Pršo and

Mikoliunas were sent off and linesman Andy Davis indicated to Hugh Dallas that a penalty should be awarded. When Fernando Ricksen stuck the penalty in the back of the net I just stood and looked up at the sky and cried as bedlam erupted around me. A couple of days after the funeral, my mum went into the Rangers shop in Falkirk and bought three identical Rangers saltire badges. We put one on my dad's grave, I kept one and she gave the other to me to keep for wee James for his first game.

Anyway, jumping forward to the last game of the season, Sunday 22nd May 2005, Celtic are at Motherwell and have all but won the league and we're away to Hibs on what looks to be a drab end to the season. Had my dad still been alive it would have been his 51st birthday. That day was also my wee cousin's first communion. My dad had been his godparent and my mum had to attend the chapel on his behalf along with the rest of the family. There was no way out of it for me so I had to go to the chapel! I had also been allocated a ticket through my season ticket so there was no doubt that I'd be going to the game but I had to make a mad dash to get to the pub on time. I remember another cousin running me to the pub after I'd changed from a shirt into my Rangers top in the chapel car park! I also pinned the badge my mum had bought onto my top which was something I hadn't done since I was in my early teens. I got into the pub about 20 minutes before we were due to leave to shouts of, "Where have you been this morning?"

I just laughed and got a beer. My mates that I go to the football with are a great bunch of guys and knew what I'd been through during the last couple of months. They also knew that day would have been my dad's 51st birthday had he still been alive.

We got through to Edinburgh in plenty of time and the

place was already busy with Bears. We got a carry-out and headed into a courtyard behind some flats at the top of Easter Road. My wee brother-in-law was also there. He was too young to drink, but he had a bottle opener on a keyring and became the most popular guy amongst the many Bears having a drink in the courtyard!

We made our way down to the stadium and watched what was really a pretty boring run-of-the-mill game. We were 1-0 up thanks to Nacho Novo and there was a few minutes to go. We knew that Celtic were winning 1-0 at Motherwell and it looked as if it was all over. Then all of a sudden another Bear in the row in front who had a radio pinned to his ear hit the roof along with others dotted around with radios. It was obvious that Motherwell had scored and we all went daft. I remember trying to phone my wife who was at my aunt and uncles' house following the first communion mentioned earlier, but I couldn't get a signal.

Then a second roar went up and I assumed it was full-time at Motherwell. Our game was still being played but all we needed to do was keep the ball for the last few seconds and the league was ours. Then the referee blew his whistle and it was party time. There were fans on the pitch and those of us in the top level went ballistic! I eventually got through to my wife who was still at my aunt and uncle's with the rest of my family. Several of my aunt's family were Celtic supporters and were absolutely gutted.

I was crying on the phone as all I could think about was my dad. My wife asked if I wanted to talk to my mum but I just couldn't. I told my wife that I'd probably go for a few beers when I got back as I was of work on the Monday. She just replied, "See you tomorrow then!"

It was only after the trophy presentation when we were

walking back up Easter Road that I found out that Celtic had been beaten 2-1. I hadn't even asked my wife what the score was!

Walking up Easter Road was great with the Bears in full song, then we could hear a car horn getting blasted behind us and a bit of a commotion. Then the crowd parted and through comes big Marvin Andrews who's out of his sunroof shaking hands with everyone. It was one of the most surreal sights I've ever seen!

We got back to the bus and some of the older guys who'd been mates with my dad are all hugging me, and I'm going on about how it would have been his birthday and they were saying that he'd sorted it for us to win! I also remember the bus arriving back in Camelon with quite a few folk outside the pubs all giving those who'd been on the bus a heroes' welcome. Most of us, however, stayed on to go to the Masonic Arms in Longcroft as we knew it would really be bouncing. We weren't disappointed and I have to say the rest of the night is a bit of a blur!

To bring the story up to date. I have kept on my dad's season ticket, changing it into my wife's name until James is old enough to use it regularly. He went to his first game on the 28th of July 2007, against Chelsea, aged 2¾ proudly wearing his Rangers top and the badge my mum bought him 2 years before.

T.Young

I've got a couple of dozen pictures from inside the stadium when the team came back to Ibrox with the trophy. However, my memory of that day is the video of the match.

My mate next door didn't have Setanta so we rigged up one of those wireless things for sending Sky to other rooms from my house to his house which worked fine until the last couple of minutes and McNee who's commentating tells us of Motherwell's equaliser. So I start channel hopping to Fir Park. Bearing in mind this was only the equaliser with still a minute or so left, my knees are wobbly, hands shaking and fingers useless. Couldn't find the channel to get back to Easter Road!

Finally get there and Motherwell score again. Start to channel hop, same result as before, almost missing full-time at Easter Road. Meanwhile my neighbour who's taking the match from my Sky box is going ballistic at my efforts... and all this has been relived over and over every time I watch Helicopter Sunday.

Diane Ward

Was working overtime that day, 0700 till 1430, but I'd received a call at work to say one of my young cousins lost his battle with cancer that morning, just a few weeks short of his 15th birthday.

My supervisor took me home straight away, and my fiancé Craig asked if I fancied going to the pub to watch the game anyway, might cheer me up a bit.

I was a bit apprehensive after the news I'd had. My cousin lived in America and I'd met him a few months earlier - he was sporty, intelligent and had so much to look forward to. His grandpa is Scottish and a Rangers fan and had all the grandkids supporting them. I thought, maybe we could go watch the game and raise a glass to the wee man.

So Craig and I set off, and went to Lock 27 in Anniesland. It was full to bursting by the time kick-off arrived. We raised our glasses to the wee man and watched the events unfold. When it came apparent Scott McDonald had scored for Motherwell, the pub just erupted! There was that chance we could have the title now, if only Motherwell could score again…

Another round of drinks and the pub was jumping, and when McDonald's second goal went in, I swear there was actually silence until the replay showed the ball hitting the back of the net. Everyone was motionless, staring towards the screens, and suddenly I was almost smothered by all these people jumping about and shouting. One guy even picked me up and spun round, it was an awesome thing to witness!

I phoned my mum (who lives in Malaysia) and started singing, "There's only one Terry Butcher," down the phone. I had to run outside and explain to my mum what had happened that day, she couldn't believe it! I told her the helicopter was changing direction and it's NOT going to Fir Park!

Eventually we staggered out of Lock 27 and ended up in town somewhere, celebrating with other fans who, like us, just couldn't believe what had happened.

What started out as a really sad day for me became one of the best days of my life. Going from those two emotions so quickly was so overwhelming I must admit I did shed a wee tear at full-time that day.

Brian Whitelaw

I live in Canada but was over visiting my mum and sister in Largs.

On that famous Sunday, me and my sister's three boys, all of us big Bluenoses of course, discussed the possibility of us being League Champions at the end of the day. Only one of us (not me) thought we would do it. We decided to go down to Potter's in Largs to see if the game was on, and to play some snooker and pool. As we walked in, the guy on the door politely informed us that only the Rangers game would be shown (good enough for us).

So we're playing snooker and watching the game, and cheered of course when we went up 1-0. To be quite honest though, we were not really focusing on the scores as we knew the other mob were winning as well.

All of a sudden, we heard the roar of the crowd through the TV, and found out Motherwell had scored. Needless to say, we stopped playing and started believing. The next few minutes was nerve wracking, watching Hibs and us play the ball around like it was a practice session. When the final whistles went, we all went absolutely nuts.

Some Tims on the next table smashed their cues over the table and stormed out. At that time, we didn't even know McDonald had scored a second goal (not that it mattered as far as the League was concerned). For me, it was a special occasion not just because we had pulled of the unbelievable, but because I got to share it with my three nephews. We hadn't all been together for a long time, and probably won't be together again for some time to come, so this made it extra special.

Ross Logie

Sunday 22nd May has arrived and I've got to get out my bed and go and watch Celtic win the league. What a great thought to start the day off.

It's straight on the phone to the boys, where we meeting? What time? Midday arrives and all the boys and I are sat in this café getting some breakfast down us before we head to the local bar, and watch the afternoon's dreaded events unfold. There was a group of 'smug' Celtic fans in there at the same time as us, all with big smiles on their faces, laughing, joking and bursting for a party. Rumour had it that the local Celtic Supporters Club had hired an open-top bus for after the game, so when they are crowned SPL Champions they can all jump on this bus and make their way through the streets celebrating. But I'll come back to that later.

Anyway, we all arrive in the pub after stuffing our faces and the place is rammed. Was there something in the air, because I was half expecting it not to be that busy with people not wanting to watch the horror that was so expected.

Did everyone believe?

To be honest, I didn't.

I decided not to drink that day, as I was going to go home as soon as the final whistle went, even planning my route so as to avoid the 'traffic' that would have been polluting the streets.

So the game kicks off and half-time arrives what seemed like 5 minutes later.

Celtic 1-0 up, and we're drawing 0-0. Typical.

My pal and I are sat down in the Lounge area, shaking the heads, coming to realise this is what it's like on the other side of that 'Last day of the Season Title Misery' syndrome.

"I've had the shitiest week ever," my mate David pipes up. "I ran someone over during the week and was late for work, so had to explain to my boss why."

As we both sit there with our arm's folded looking at the floor, my reply is, "It's about to get worse," or so we thought.

We make our way back into the bar, and stand with the rest of the Bears in our usual spot.

Yessss, Novo gets the goal, but not too much of a celebration that would normally follow a goal against Hibs to make it 1-0. The minutes are going past in double quick time, as are the Irn-Brus.

Still 1-0 to Celtic at Fir Park and surely it's just a matter of time before we hear Gerry McNee utter the words, "2-0 at Fir Park."

That would have been my cue to go home and try to forget about this horrible day.

"And there's been a goal at Fir Park," (there it was, my cue to leave, put the Irn-Bru down, say cheerio, and leave)… was that a roar from the Bears?… or was it the Hibees noising us up?

"Scott McDonald has equalised."

There was a slight moment of confusion and excitement at the same time, was this true? Surely not? Can it be?

The screen splits into two showing us McDonald's goal… YESSSSSSS!

Bedlam everywhere, people jumping on my back, hugging me… and Joe kissing everyone as always!

But it wasn't over, I removed myself from the bar and got myself into the lounge. I couldn't celebrate yet, I had to know for 100% that the title was ours.

The clock hit 90:00, and what felt like the longest 2 minutes of my life unfolded. I was shaking, sweating, and trying to block out the roars of jubilation coming from next door… then the moment that will live with me till my death bed. McLeish makes that sign with his hands that it's all over at Fir Park, and that was it, we were the SPL Champions. I was back in the bar in around 0.4 seconds, sprinting past the two coppers and back in amongst the bedlam that was happening. People you barely knew were hugging you, shaking your hand. The champagne comes out and the walls are covered in it. I make the call to Australia to my mate Andy, who is on his travels and at something like 3am he's on the sofa waiting to see what the outcome is. I can't imagine what went through his head when he saw my name appear on his phone and then heard the pub in full voice after answering!

To be honest, I can't remember what was said, and I wasn't even drunk... yet! My phone was passed round a few times and, to be honest, I wasn't caring, it was only Australia!

Next minute the whole place is out on the street causing rather a large traffic jam with everyone doing the bouncy in the middle of the road. God knows what they were all thinking! The beers started flowing and the night becomes that little bit too blurry to remember, but I do remember it was a good night and shall be remembered for the rest of my days!

The day after was probably the best hangover I've ever had in my life! I still get the hairs standing up and a lump in the throat every time I hear that roar, and the scenes on the DVD when the final whistle is blown is amazing.

I wonder if the Jersey CSC got their money back for the open-top bus?

Russell Telfer

The day before, I had arranged to meet my mate in the New Regent for the game at 1:30. On the Sunday my pal called me at 1:40 to see where I was. I was in a bit of a mess as I'd been up till about six the night before drinking. I told him I was too rough and couldn't make it. We then had a big argument, him saying, "Don't be lazy, you never know what might happen."

Anyway, I scraped myself out of bed and made the way down to the pub feeling and looking like a burst couch. Got to the pub which was mobbed and tucked in to a pint. Rangers went one up and we watched the game, sinking as many pints as I could trying and sort myself out a bit.

Then suddenly the bar door burst open. "It's one each!" a guy shouts.

Everyone is wondering, is this guy on the wind-up? Then it came up on the telly, the place erupted, pints in the air, everyone jumping about like mad. Then the second went in.

Woof!

Again, jumping about mad, covered in beer but ecstatic and overjoyed.

When the final whistle went on the Rangers game it felt like forever for the Motherwell game to finish.

After the game we made our way down to the Angel on Paisley Road to celebrate and meet our pals who were at the game. Paisley Road was buzzing, the pub was mobbed and we partied well in to the night.

My last memory of the night was sitting in a corner outside a taxi rank thinking, I can't believe I was going to stay in bed.

What a day!

Andrew McCrae

I live in Edinburgh (albeit nowhere near Easter Road) but didn't have a ticket and didn't bother calling in favours to get one as I thought we had no chance. Anyway, day of the match I wandered up to the local pub which, as the only known Hibee pub in the area, was showing our game on the big screen and the Tims game on a wee portable courtesy of Arab TV. The pub was mobbed with Hibees who even after we scored weren't bothered as long as they got into Europe. Cue the two McDonald goals and about 3-4 Bears in the pub going mad.

After the final whistle I went outside and called a taxi

informing the controller I wanted to go to Easter Road. When the taxi driver shows up he asks if I'm on the wind-up.

"Nope," says I.

"Good," says he, adding, "I'm a Jambo and after what they Tims done to us against St Mirren in the 80s, it'll be my pleasure to get you as close and as quickly as possible." Fifteen minutes later after a mad dash across town he drops me off on Easter Road itself. I strolled purposefully through the police cordon and straight into the now deserted main stand as if I owned the place. Nobody batted an eyelid. Arrived just in time to see the trophy being presented and the celebrations begin. Of course, being in the main stand I was away from the mass celebrations (although there was a couple of undercover Bears of my acquaintance already there) but that had its own benefits; I not only had a great view but the freedom to roam around. As a result I can truthfully claim to be the last person to talk to Ricksen as he left the field with the trophy - with him bringing the league trophy over personally to show me and a couple of other lads just before he disappeared up the tunnel. All in all a good day out.

The epilogue to this story begins about an hour later and involves an Edinburgh pub (the Hebrides Bar, if my memory serves me right). Me and a number of other (mostly Edinburgh-based) Bears singing down the phone to Terry Butcher on his mobile…

Billy Halliday

I had been living in New Zealand for over a year and used to listen to and watch the games live at home in Queenstown over the internet. I had watched several matches, staying up till the wee small hours. On occasions if the pub was quiet, or nothing was happening in town, I would head home early to catch the game. May is the quietest month of the year in Queenstown.

On the 22nd May 2005, and early morning 23rd I decided to do just that, home time it was. I wasn't looking forward to it as I fully accepted that the title was heading to the opposite end of Glasgow, and remembered the now famous Celtic banner at Ibrox a few weeks earlier, 'We won the league at Ibrox 5 points clear' on a snow-dropped bed sheet.

The last thing I wanted to listen to after a disappointing night out was them talk on Clyde Super Scoreboard about Celtic winning against Motherwell.

I settled down just before kick off with the radio on and surfing the Internet, mostly on followfollow.com, having a few joints and another beer. I wasn't really interested in what was going on, not really listening, it was like I just put it on for the background atmosphere, probably just a habit.

The second half kicked off and I decided enough was enough, it was time to get the head down and get some shut eye with Rangers 1-0 up and the same scoreline at Fir Park. I had convinced myself that Celtic would again (it's Motherwell they're playing) win the league and I put the lights out, with Clyde still going on in the background.

It took a few seconds to sink in, but I really did think I was dreaming. But after having a reality check I soon knew this was for real and immediately jumped up, so fast it was like I was being dragged out of bed tied to a sports car.

It was on, there was hope. Big Marvin Andrews came in to my head straight away from the comments that were laughed at through the media previously.

I started shouting and going nuts, opened the balcony doors and shouted, "Come on the Gers, come on Motherwell". My neighbour, a West Ham fan who I met over there, heard this and, as he was not exactly in close proximity, he phoned me to see what was going on. While on the phone a certain Mr McDonald popped up again and it was 2-1 Motherwell.

I went absolutely nuts myself, alone, jumped over the couch, ran out the door, ran up the street, cheering and repeatedly shouting, "YES! YES! YA FUCKING BEAUTY! YEEE HAAA."

There was nobody around, I was lost, I didn't know what to do, no one to tell. I have celebrated many times but this was one of the weirdest experiences I have ever had. Celebrating on my own in total shock. If anyone had seen me that night they would have called an ambulance or the doctors with the white coats.

It was a few minutes later my mate arrived and we opened the chilled beers that were in the fridge. I texted a few others to tell what had just happened and see if they were awake at this time in the morning. Within 45 minutes our title party was in full swing. Another three Bears celebrated and three others appeared so that I was not celebrating alone. They were West Ham, Leeds and Chelsea fans. We later had the tunes playing from Calton Radio and my CDs were back on.

My boss arrived at 8:45am to see where I was. I just completely forgot that I was working that day at 7:30am. I told him what happened and he totally understood the situation even though he's a Kiwi who loves rugby.

"No excuses, we won the league in the last minute and we had to celebrate the way it was won," I said.

After listening to the story, of which he was oblivious to the facts, he laughed and said, "OK, see you in the morning, enjoy the day!"

As a scaffolder, I took a 6m (21ft) tube from the truck

parked at home and put my St Andrew's flag on the top, fastened to my balcony. **The tunes were on and the flag was raised.**

From that morning, half the town, people I knew and didn't know, got to know me as 'that mad Scottish Rangers fan with the flag'. It was like a socialising exercise, after that night more people wanted to know more about me and the mighty Glasgow Rangers.

The flag became famous as it could be seen in most of the town.

I continued partying at my place until around 11am and headed down to the pub for more refreshments and a sing-song.

Believe it or not, my address when in New Zealand was Antrim Street... directly at the top of Glasgow Street.

A day that will live with me for ever and remind me of one of the greatest places on earth. That's how I experienced that day, one minute I was feeling down, bored, and a few minutes later I'm having a celebratory party with a few friends that continued for around 14 hours on the sauce.

James MacDonald

The following events get a little blurry in places but the thought of that day still gives me shivers. The location chosen for the day was The Auctioneers pub just off George Square.

After losing to Celtic at Ibrox a couple of weeks earlier were still causing grief at work. But slowly and surely the lead at the top was crumbling. Still, any talk of confidence in us winning the league was more bravado than common sense.

My Helicopter Sunday

I had been watching the Setanta games in the Auctioneers throughout the season so, confident in the partisan crowd, I decided that was the best location. The general feeling of 'it would be too good to be true' was happening, and one by one my viewing buddies were dropping out. But more in need of a beer to settle my nerves than through confidence I went on my tod to watch the game.

The minutes were not flying past but as the day wore on it was becoming more apparent that the 'others' were bricking it too.

Nacho scored!

Different ball game now, and the lager fuelled mathematicians were in full stat analysis mode to confirm exactly what was needed. Not long before the shoes and socks came off to start using the toes to count, the word started to spread that Motherwell had scored. It was as if as soon as you heard you did one jump of celebration, but before you had landed from the first bounce you had started asking, "Are you sure?"

Word was spreading, texts were flying, some believed (thanks Marvin), some didn't. Then in the corner of the screen it showed the goal from Fir Park, and now you could celebrate. It was hard jumping in celebration, only with your mates you only met an hour or so ago, and still with clenched buttocks, still nervous about the outcome. It was close now, and still kind of thinking, surely no… we weren't going to pull it off were we?

Clock watching was being taken to Olympic standards, when a wee speccy chef with the funny checked trousers ran full pelt fom the kitchen. He was chuffed about something, then started shouting, "GOAL AT FIR PARK!"

At this point the boozer was firmly split 50/50. One half

wanted to kill him, assuming he was winding us right up and gloating that Celtic had equalised. The other was laughing at him saying that was what we have all been celebrating for the last five minutes.

I never heard his exact words, but the ripple started there and beer started flying, emanating from that point. IT WAS ANOTHER FOR MOTHERWELL!

Celebrate when the news was heard, celebrate some more when they confirmed on telly, celebrate another bit more when the pictures of the second goal come in… count the seconds! Seeing the helicopter turn you didn't know what to do. Just kinda laugh, celebrate, shake your head, it still didn't seem real.

Finally the whistle went, and it was still sinking in. Celebration time, and you were jumping with your new best mates. Songs were being belted out, phones were up in the air trying to relay the atmosphere for those who stayed away. He might not be the favourite son anymore, but when Terry Butcher came on TV for his interview afterwards a collective silence fell. You just knew he was loving it!

Murdo McLennan

I was in the second year of my degree at Aberdeen University at the time of Helicopter Sunday. Couldn't make the game as I was studying, as were a lot of my Rangers-supporting mates at the time. But we'd all arranged to meet at our student pub (around 50 of us by the way) and watch the game together. This pub is just up from Pittodrie but it's packed with student Bears whenever we have a game on the TV. Game was split, upstairs had the Celtic match (for the Tims, and Aberdeen fans) and downstairs was for the Rangers fans (we outnumbered them at least 2:1 that day).

Anyways, on the way to the pub I got a call from my uncle, who goes to pretty much every match, for a chat about the game. I'm not afraid to admit I wasn't confident, but thought that 'something might happen'.

My uncle is usually a bit downbeat about Rangers going into games, but not that day, he was very, very confident that we were going to do it. Unusually so in fact. It really did set the tone for the day.

Tims score and we're getting dogs' abuse from upstairs from the fans; the downstairs of the pub, where we all were, got very quiet and sombre. Cue Nacho Novo and we erupted, it was back on.

Channels were then split all over the pub, so both games were on at the same time. Cue Scott McDonald. Don't think I've ever seen anything like the mayhem that ensued when he scored the first. Rangers fans everywhere hugging, up on tables, beer getting thrown around, tables all over the place, something I'll never forget. Then the second went in, same again. Just about the happiest I've ever been in my 22 years on this planet. To be so unconfident before the game, and just to realise what in fact had happened, those feelings will live with me for ever. At full-time we started to sing all the old party favourites, and we made sure that the Tims had a hard time getting out of the pub (as the only way out was through us!)

As for my uncle, I remember him calling me after the game, when we were all walking back to a 'wee' sash bash at my pal's. All he said was, "We are the people," and hung up.

What a day, which we'll probably never see the likes of again.

David Welsh

Saturday night before the game. Me and my best mate decide we are going to travel to the capital and chance our luck at getting into the ground. I was 16 at the time and both our dads and other mates decided to slate us, calling us idiots and saying we were wasting our money going to the game. Oh how wrong they were.

Can't remember the exact times but we got up fairly early and headed into Glasgow City Centre to get the train. I remember us both sitting on the train not saying a word to each other because of nerves. My stomach was churning. I remember clearly bowing my head on the train and praying to God that this would be a glorious day. I hadn't prayed for about two years when I used to attend church regularly. But God answered my call that day!

We arrived in Edinburgh and spent about an hour trying to find the stadium. We must have walked by it around 5 times not noticing it because of the tenement houses. Eventually we found the stadium. We saw the team arrive and wished a few of them all the best. Later on Klos arrived in his car with a few of the injured players in the squad. We had a chat with them and also wished them all the best.

Time was running out faster and faster before kick off and we still hadn't got a ticket. About half an hour before the game we decided if we ran back to the train station we could get back to the Rosevale pub in Partick and try to get in there to watch the game. Halfway along the road I decided, "Feck this, I have my radio. Worse comes to worse we will sit outside Easter Road and listen to it on that."

So again we walked back down to Easter Road. There was 5 minutes to kick off and there was this huge guy who was pretty scary standing with two tickets. We asked him if we could have them, to be told new piss off they were for mates. Cue two guys kitted out in Burberry coming up behind us and taking the tickets off him!

That was our last chance. Or so we thought. Somehow I decided to ask the guy that just bought the tickets if he had any spare. He just laughed and walked away. Then shouted, "Wait!" and came back over. He dug deep into his Stone Island jacket and pulled out a ticket for the Rangers end marked Hibs v Rangers, November(I think) 2002. He told me he got the jail before that game and gave me the ticket for free. Me and my mate ran as fast as we could to the turnstile and tried getting in with the one ticket.

We got huckled out. Our chance of seeing the game was well and truly over.

Then a guy comes banging into us and we asked him for a ticket, we got one for in the Hibs end. My mate Scott takes the one for the Hibs end and I make my way to the turnstile, shitting myself in case I get caught for having an out-of-date ticket.

It worked and soon as I got through I ran straight to the toilets to hide. After about two minutes of calming myself down I decided to head to try to get a seat. I saw some young guys coming in and asked if I could squeeze in because I didn't have a ticket. Much to my delight they let me. I would like to say thank you to them and to the guy for the out-of-date ticket!

Anyway, I remember getting a seat and just being so nervous it was unreal. I felt like spewing. The game also seemed to be going really fast! All sorts of situations were spinning in my head.

Celtic score and all you hear are the Hibs fans cheering. Eventually when the Gers scored through wee Novo I went ballistic for about a minute then sat straight back down again. It was a weird celebration because we knew we still needed Celtic to slip up!

There was about 5 minutes to go and no one around me was watching the game. We were all looking at the old fella listening to his radio to see what happened. "Wait," he says, then jumps up shouting, "Motherwell have scored!"

From there on in it was nuts, me and the guy behind me were cuddling and crying with tears of joy. Then about 2 minutes later we were all going nuts again. I thought it was just full-time, I didn't know that wee Scott McDonald had scored another. When the full-time whistle went everyone ran on the pitch. I decided to join in on the fun. I ran to wee Novo who was up in the air getting lifted by some guys. I grabbed his leg and was screaming and shouting. He must have felt it because I was making my grip tighter and tighter. Sorry Novo! Then the police came out with shields and horses, and I shat myself and ran back and jumped the wall into the stand!

I just remember being so happy and receiving hundreds of texts saying, "I can see you on Setanta". And my reply, "I told you so," to all the unbelievers who said that we wouldn't do it.

I remember seeing Big Marvin's T-shirt and nearly crying with happiness at what it said. It summed up the day for me.

After the celebrations it was out to find my mate who had actually made his way round to the Gers end once the game was over to celebrate we ran at each other and sort of leapt into a cuddle and we both fell screaming and cuddling on the ground!

Then it was back to the train. We met a bunch of older guys who had a carry-out and kindly shared it with us while we had a sing-song on the way home to Glasgow. From town we went straight to Partick to meet our dads where we all went nuts outside the Rosevale for about 20 minutes. We tried getting in but were asked for ID, so we jumped a taxi and headed over to Ibrox for more singing and celebrations. We ended up staying out most of the night back in Partick. Outside the pub for a while then up to mine to celebrate and sing some more.

It was, and still is, the best day of my life!

It will never be forgotten. God was behind us that day and we did it.

Sam English

Woke up on the Sunday morning thinking to myself, I wish the day was over, as I honestly never thought we'd actually win the title that day, never in a million years. I had arranged to meet a couple of mates to watch the game in the pub. The wife was working that afternoon and I had told her I'd have the Sunday dinner ready for when she had finished work. Off to the pub I go at one o'clock, shouting to the wife as I left, "I'll be home in a couple of hours."

When we arrived at the pub, the place was heaving, and the buzz about the place was electric. I couldn't believe that people thought it was still possible for us to win the league. I just couldn't get 'in the mood'.

The pub became that busy that by half-time we got a taxi to another pub who were showing the Rangers game. Rangers winning 1-0, Celtic winning 1-0. I was wishing it was full-time so I could just get home and try to forget about it.

With less than five minutes remaining, my mate, who had bet a guy in the pub at the start of the season £200 that Rangers would win the title, had the money in his hand to pay off his bet as we were just going to leave. Seconds later the place just erupted, Scott McDonald scored for

Motherwell. At this point Bears were up on the tables singing and dancing, so it's back to the bar for more drink, when McDonald scores again... Rangers are the Champions.

I just couldn't believe what was happening, the place was going mad. People who five minutes ago had faces that were tripping them, were now like party animals.

That was the start of a night of celebration that lasted into the wee sma' hours of the next morning.

As for the wife returning from work expecting to find her dinner on the table... she knew there was no chance of that happening.

Rab Howitt

I was due to go on a training course in Edinburgh on the Monday morning. I hadn't secured a ticket and really believed that Sunday was a formality. We would win and Celtic would win.

I resigned myself to sitting in the living room, with the radio on, and was reading a PlayStation 2 magazine with my son (12) deciding what game to buy next for us.

As expected, Celtic scored and that was that, or so I thought.

Oh ye of little faith!

At half-time, Celtic were 1-0 up and we were drawing 0-0. My parents were in the Caribbean on a cruise with my aunt and uncle, who is a Celtic supporter, and I had decided that at full-time I would send my dad a text letting him know what happened and let him enjoy the rest of his holiday as best he could. As fate would have it, wee Novo scored and suddenly the embers of a season where we had blown it were slowly re-ignited. With my ears pricking up and paying a wee bit more attention to the radio.

My Helicopter Sunday

Unexpectedly, Scott McDonald then equalised for the Steelmen, and all of a sudden the PlayStation 2 magazine was binned and I started getting the old 'wobbly knees' and daring to start 'believing' in the impossible. No sooner had I regained my composure, and wee McDonald had scored again. I ran from the living room out the back door, into the back garden, and roared, "YYYEEEEEESSSSSSSSSSSSSS!" at the top of my voice, whilst my surrounding neighbourhood was deathly silent.

By the time I got my trembling frame back into the house it was over. Done and dusted. WE were champions and Celtic were runners-up.

I found it so hard to comprehend, when my phone rang and it was my best mate, John, who had been doing the same. John and I have watched Rangers in numerous places together. I had to hang up as I was unable to speak due to nerves and crying and laughing, ALL at the same time.

My sister, who was at work in Stobhill, phoned and I was speaking to her, and she said a lot of Celtic fans in her ward were unable to get the day off on holiday. I replied, "Well it would have been a waste of a day's holiday for the Yahoos because we are the champions and they're not. First is everything, second is nothing."

It was around this point my sister informed me that I was on the 'conference' phone in the ward and EVERYONE could hear me. I didn't care, as we were champions for the 51st time in our illustrious history, and Celtic were runners-up again.

After saying our goodbyes, my thoughts turned to informing my dad with the following:

"Dad.....Hibs 0 Rangers 1...........Motherwell 2 Them 1.................We ARE the champions
AGAIN !!.............51 .....Yir Boy"

I got one back from my dad saying: "You're at it, surely?? ......WTF happened?"

I returned with: "The Yahoos capitulated and their bottle went. Enjoy!!"

It took me an age to sleep and I made sure that I bought as many newspapers as I could carry on the Monday morning. I was told our course started at 9am and I was there at 0850. I was then told it was actually 10am it started, so I got an hour to read, gloat and digest the papers. Our instructor was late. It turned out SHE had been at Easter Road and was celebrating until 0630 that morning.

As a Bluenose of 30-odd years, it was even more exciting than the season where Celtic were winning the 'Quadruple' and finished empty-handed.

Paul Cameron

One of my mates chucked the season after the last home game. So I went to the bus on my tod. I was waiting to get picked up and one of the lads states that his daughter woke up and stated she dreamt Rangers won the league as Motherwell beat Sellik. Taking it as a sign he duly bet money on this with Rangers and the winners of the Aberdeen/Hearts game as a treble.

Nothing unusual really about the journey or the pints in the pub before the game. The talk was ifs, buts and maybes with the agreement that all we could do was win our game and see. After all, it would have been a boot in the baws if Sellik did come a cropper and we failed in our bit.

The game starts and it is not a classic and you find out early that Sutton has scored for Celtic. However, we were there to follow, follow and to keep believing so we continued to belt out our encouragement.

So wee Nacho scores and the job is done at our end.

Hibs aren't interested in scoring in case we were to, as goal difference could wreck their own Euro bid. So the game is a stroll like the West Germany v Austria WC game of 1982 with everyone happy (apart from the Algerians in 1982).

So it is 15 mins of surreal times. Some people not realising things, want us to try more and have to be advised that our job here is done.

Now I'll always remember false stories filtering through from years gone by on fake scores and sending offs etc. so usually take anyone advising of events from elsewhere with a pinch of salt until I can confirm myself.

NOT THIS TIME.

There is one unified roar. It can only mean one thing and it does. The feeling is one that unless you are there cannot be described. People may have had similar in their home, pub, club or wherever they were watching it but it can only be ten fold actually at Easter Road.

Goose-bumps now just thinking back.

It is a berserk time but beautiful at the same time. However, I calm down as I know these chunts only need to score themselves to win the SPL and we look like right tits with video replays for evermore of our dashed hopes on YouTube.

One of the guys states 4 mins left.

FUCK! 4 minutes. It is electric in the stand. Every guy with a tranny or mobile phone has 4,5 maybe more mates and new mates hanging around, for what seems an eternity.

BANG!

It would be interesting to know what the power generated from the explosion of that second roar was. Thing is I thought the game had finished at Fir Park. Took me a long time after the final whistle to find out Well had scored again.

Party. Party. Party. We are going to party.

The wait is a sweet feeling. That wait for the final whistle. Marvin is giving thanks to God on the park. Alex Rae is a jack-in-the-box. Then the whistle goes and the whole explosion of joy comes out from the stand and meets the joy from the players and staff in what amounts to a love-in between them and the fans lucky enough to be on the pitch. The TV cameras cannot do it justice.

At the time I praised the police as they kept the fans apart, as one or two Hibs numpties took exception, and after a while got everyone off and back in their places without any arrests that I could see.

The rest is a wait after it calms down with Hibs players coming on and being roundly applauded by both sets of fans. And when we are finally presented it is a bit flat to me as it took ages for the trophy to arrive.

The funniest bit was after the game. We drove up Calton Hill and even though we knew Plod let us go on when we gave it the 'we are tourists' routine. So we were allowed to go down along Princes Street, instead of having to leave the normal way around the south of the city, where this happens:

We are stopped at traffic lights near the station and we spot 2 Sellik fans who as yet have not spotted us on the bus. The street is mobbed and I still think with the look of dejection on their faces that their conversation was along these lines:

"Fuck it Declan how did that happen? We are going to take some pounding in work tomorrow."

"Ah know Liam. At least the Huns go the long way home and there is no chance we will bump into any of… fuck!"

Just at that minute they looked up and spied us and we just tore right into them, banging on the windows, yelling the banter, the lot. The whole bus was rocking from side to side.

Comedy classic. One actually gave a rueful smile and nodded. A sweet, sweet moment.

Head home after going by Murrayfield where the Heineken rugby final was just finishing. Who knows what they thought of the shenanigans on our wee bus. Ibrox for the team's victory parade, where I met the wife and youngest, and then home where I had not one drink. I was mentally drained and happy.

David Goodfellow

A day I would class only inferior to the birth of my son. I had been trying frantically to get a ticket as I always had a slight glimmer of hope that something could happen. And if not I wanted to cheer on the team I love for one final time that season. On the Saturday night I discovered that my friend Iain had got me a ticket and that there would be three of us travelling through as one of the boys could not go due to work commitments. As we travelled through to the east coast we discussed the chance that we would take our glorious trawl of titles to 51 and my two friends, Craig and Iain, were adamant that this was going to be our day… although in all honesty I was not too sure.

We arrived in the capital 45 minutes before kick off. Although we had all been to Easter Road before we still managed to get lost. As we parked up and ran to the ground and climbed the steep steps in the lower section my phone beeped as the Uddingston Bus convenor, Billy, took great pleasure in noticing we were ten minutes late in arriving into the game.

As I arrived in my seat, thankfully on the aisle, I had a smile on my face as I saw a Rangers legend was next to me, Stuart McCall. Excellent touch to the day as he was always one of my heroes.

The game plodded on as Novo put us ahead and we had heard that Celtic had scored too and were on their way to the title. A guy in front, who I believe was Chris Burke's dad, was listening on the tranny and keeping us updated with what was going on. The next few minutes are a complete haze of ecstasy, disbelief and overall joy. The guy in front jumped up screaming we have done it, as the whole stand rocked and I was pushed 3 seats along and 2 rows forward. I realised something great had happened although word had not spread as to what exactly happened and then just as I heard McDonald had scored. The next thing a second roar went up which we found out was not the final whistle at Fir Park as we thought but McDonald's second!

I will never forget the celebrations after that as we waited for the helicopter to change direction and travel to Edinburgh. Also a very strange sight seeing many grown men cry in happiness! My mobile constantly vibrated as Setanta were kind enough to make my day even more memorable as they had my ugly mug on the screen for long periods as we celebrated. Very much to do with who was standing near me as previously mentioned.

Travelling home to Uddingston I still don't think it had completely registered and it would take a couple of days to really hit home. But once it did, anytime I talk of that day, the hairs stand up on the back of my neck! As a great man said on the 22nd May 2005, "Keep believing."

Peter Keenan

Was in Lanzarote sitting on the beach when I got a text asking how I was enjoying the match. I quickly made my excuses to the wife, kids and mother (babysitter, why not?) and shuffled my way to the nearest bar, Totty McHowkers or something of this ilk. Saw a huge screen as I walked in the door with only sky and clouds showing! I asked the nearest and only person, may I add, watching the screen what was happening and was met with, "I no know I only smoke pipe."

Okey-dokey, straight to the empty bar. Same question to Irish barmaid, "Hi, what's happening with the football?"

Her retort, "Those Rangers bastards have only won the league."

"Two pints please, and one for yourself."

Quaffing second pint when the proprietor appears (big, friendly, genial Irishman). His comment, "Right, turn off all those TVs we're shut."

Mmmm sweet! Bye Now!

David Griffiths

In the house alone on a sunny Sunday in Cheshire, the missus and kiddies out for a family lunch. As I had stood them up to watch the football, I was left to iron the clothes for our holiday the next week. There I was, slaving over a hot iron with the TV on behind me.

Setanta screened both Hibs v Rangers and Motherwell v Celtic games on different channels. I watched the Rangers game for the first half and heard from Setanta that Celtic had scored. Kept watching the Rangers game until Novo scored then, realising all it took was a Motherwell goal, switched to the Tims game. Couldn't stomach watching the filth winning so I kept flicking back to Easter Road.

With 20 minutes to go, a fellow Bear who wasn't watching sent me a text asking, "No change? Any chance, you think?" I sent one back saying, "No chance, forget it." 2 or 3 minutes to go, I watched as Motherwell launched a hopeful ball forward. When it was headed clear, I switched over in despair. Seconds later, a roar starts to build and build and BUILD at Easter Road. McNee says, "And the Rangers fans are cheering..." Surely not. It can't be. Can it? "Motherwell have equalised!" says McNee. I turn over to see the Motherwell players hugging at the corner flag.

With iron in one hand and phone in the other, I phone my text mate, my hand shaking so much I can't keep the phone still. When he answers, I blurt out, "You're not gonna believe this, they've equalised!"

He says, "What? Who's equalised, Hibs?"

"No, Motherwell!" I tell him. I then commentate down the phone as McDonald hares downfield, cuts inside and sends a deflected looper into the far corner. "YES!" I scream down the phone. "We've won the fucking league!"

I set up the tape for the post-match celebrations and head off to the family do, which is my wife's gran's 98th birthday party. Two fellow-Bears phone me from Ibrox as the unplanned victory celebrations start. When I walk in to the pub, her cousin, a Leeds fan, walks over to congratulate me. Totally impromptu, I jump on him and dance round the room! I buy a round for the assembled party, including two bottles of champagne. A £58 round, worth every penny. Sadly, her gran died a few weeks later but at least I made an old lady smile on her last birthday.

I kept my mate's text for months after as a reminder never to give up, even if all seems lost, or as Big Marv said, "Keep believing."

Greig Knox

As you are aware, it was the last weekend of the season. Rangers were playing catch-up most of the year. Celtic were stuttering towards the title and everyone including myself and my 4 mates, who are diehard Bears, didn't think we would win the league; if only we had listened to Big Marv!

As we all know, Rangers had all but thrown away the title race after losing 2-1 at Ibrox against Celtic. Celtic fans even produced banners at that game claiming to be champions.

Victories over Aberdeen, Hearts and Motherwell followed, but only the most optimistic supporter thought the Gers could still win the league. Rangers needed a poor Motherwell side to beat Celtic at Fir Park, while the Light Blues had to negotiate a tricky away tie at Easter Road against a Hibs side on course for a UEFA Cup spot.

As it looked a formality that Celtic would win the league, we decided to take our wives away for a weekend in Manchester, which happened to coincide with a Neil Diamond concert; honest! Anyway, part of the deal was that we would get to the airport very early on the Sunday morning, to claim the best seats in the bar and to ensure that it was the Rangers game that they were showing.

Well the weekend was a riot and things went to plan on the Sunday morning. Me and my mates got to the bar nice and early, just in case there were any Tims lurking about trying to get their game on; after all you still want to watch the Rangers no matter what. We got the best seats in the bar and we sat down to watch the game.

Just as the game started, we spotted a Celtic fan enter the bar in the only clothes that they seem to have, i.e. a green and grey hoopy number for those fortunate enough to have never came across them.

It didn't look good early on; Nacho Novo missed an open goal from a tight angle while Chris Sutton put Celtic 1-0 up at Fir Park. As the second half dragged on, what hope remained amongst the Rangers supporters began to fade. With minutes to go in each game, both Rangers and Celtic were holding a one goal lead. Then a long ball from Motherwell eventually finds its way to Scott McDonald. The Aussie, with his back to goal, hits a fantastic shot over his left shoulder and it sails into the net.

Easter Road erupts.

As the final seconds of the Rangers game ticked away, the news filtered through that Scott McDonald had doubled Motherwell's lead in the space of a few minutes. The victory was secured, the most dramatic Scottish Championship win was secured, the helicopter changed direction.

William Watt

My mate and I had not managed to get to an away match all season. As it was a forgone conclusion that the Tims would slaughter Motherwell, there were 2 of our supporters club's tickets going spare. So off we set and drove up from Blackpool to Edinburgh to watch the game.

With around 10 minutes to go I turned to my mate and said, "We will just wait until the final whistle, give the team a hard luck round of applause and make our way back."

The rest is, of course, history. I managed to speed back to Blackpool in two and a half hours and went on a mega celebration.

Harry Brooks

The build up to that day was listening to the Tims and the sheep give me a hard time at work. Even some Rangers men were all doom and gloom. But as the weekend got closer I began to think something was going to happen. The Tims, as normal, got over-confident and I thought to myself, if Rangers beat Hibs, and Celtic are not a couple of goals ahead of Motherwell, then we still have a chance. I began telling the Bears at work not to worry as I really think we will do it. Some of them said, "No way", and I told them to remember our song, *No Surrender*.

On the Friday our Tim boss was so happy and he told me he does not expect to see me on Monday as I will be off crying. I replied that I will be off on Monday but I will be celebrating and I look forward to seeing him on Tuesday. He laughed and I thought, just you wait.

Come Sunday, I left the house to walk into Aberdeen city centre to a bar called The Metro. It was owned by a Rangers supporter and he put the big screen on so we could watch the game.

As I passed through the shopping centre and JJB sports I saw the new Rangers top in the window. I had no intention of buying it yet as I thought, if I buy it now and things went wrong I would never forget it. Then I thought, no way are we going to blow it today. I bought the top and went on to watch the game.

A couple of pints with some friends and the Rangers kicked off. The Tims 1-0 up and Rangers 1-0 up. Thinking, come on Motherwell please, just one goal. A big roar went up and on the screen Scott McDonald had made it 1-1. The place was bouncing, and I mean bouncing. Fucking brilliant. I knew it. I knew we would win the League today, I knew we could do it. Another roar went up and I thought that was it, all over. I didn't even know McDonald scored again till later on that night.

It's time to party. I partied until my mates that were at the game arrived back in Aberdeen. We met up and had a fantastic time, drink after drink after drink.

Made it home in the early hours of Monday morning determined to go to work and get stuck into all those Tims and sheep. But I was still drunk, so sadly could not make it into work until Tuesday. I've never been so happy to go to work in all my life like that day. As soon as I got in I gave them hell, I did not shut up all day and the Tim boss was not a happy chappie. I tore into about him at every chance, and even if he sacked me he would never have stopped me smiling. I was in Heaven and it was because of my team The Rangers.

On Wednesday the Tim boss told me to 'fuck up' as it's all done now so give over. I told him to 'fuck up' himself as I have listened to him all season and now he has all summer to listen to me.

What a lovely summer.

I have had some wonderful times following the Rangers but that was something else. A day I will never forget. WE ARE THE PEOPLE.

Paul Cameron

My pal is the manager of Dixons in Glasgow Airport and one of his staff (Frank doesn't work Sundays) told him that the Sellik shop, with about ten minutes to final whistle, had all these boxes stacked up and started opening them and putting the merchandise on the railings for the passengers to browse and purchase.

However, round about full-time one of their staff gets a call on the phone and the one way conversation is along the lines of:

"Whit?"

"Tell me yer fuckin' joking!"

"Aw naw."

"Right."

He then comes off the phone all ashen-looking and starts shouting to the rest of the staff:

"Get them back in the boxes. NOW!"

Apparently this merchandise had messages on it proclaiming 'Sellik SPL champs 2005'.

OOOPS!

Scott Ricardson

I was working on the rigs in Russia at the time and on the morning of the game I was flying from western Siberia to south-west Russia. I had a 6-hour layover in Domodedovo Airport in Moscow. I sat at the bar and spoke to family and friends on my mobile throughout the morning with the main subject being the game. Some were going to it, most were watching it, but nearly all were resigned to the Tims being able to beat Motherwell to win the league. Being the eternal optimist, I was telling everybody that I was confident that we would beat the Hibees and maybe, just maybe, the Steelmen would do us the favour of all favours. I had been speaking to Motherwell fans I knew and knew that they would just love to spoil the Tims party.

I was going to be flying when the game was on and would be landing in Astrakhan in south-west Russia just as the games would be due to end. By the time I landed in Astrakhan I was well oiled having taken advantage of the in-flight hospitality. I called my brother-in-law's house where I knew there were a few watching it, including my brother and father-in-law. When the phone was answered, all I could hear was the sound of sheer celebration. The final whistle had just blown and all these grown men were hugging, dancing and running around the living room. I spoke to my brother and I could hardly understand his insane garbling, he was so ecstatic. He was telling me that when McDonald scored his first goal there were at least 2 drinks spilled on the ceiling of the living room. I then spoke with my father-in-law and he couldn't talk for crying.

So there was me, in a little backwater airport in southern Russia jumping about with my hands in the air. I was probably the only English-speaking person in the arrival lounge and they probably thought I was off my head.

I was met by a driver who I instructed to head straight for a shop where I could buy some celebratory beer. I then spent the 2-hour journey calling anybody and everybody I knew and singing Rangers songs at the top of my voice. The driver thought it was hilarious.

That was my day of Helicopter Sunday and I will never forget it.

David Lancaster

Was working in Paris for a couple of years and whilst there kept up my Sky/Setanta accounts. However, as luck would have it, I ended up in a small town in SW France far from my illegally-placed satellite dish on that fateful day. My work was pretty intense for this 3-week period of displacement which included working weekends. I was in charge, so had to be seen to be doing the business!

My Helicopter Sunday

On Saturday we had the official day out in Toulouse, the pink city. I started thinking – Stade Français (Paris) v Stade Toulousain in Edinburgh in the Rugby Heineken Cup Final. I'm in Toulouse, a Paris dweller, whose team was playing a team in Edinburgh... mmmmm... nah, forget it!

Anyway, Sunday came, and my wife, who had come down from Paris for the weekend, had to leave Agen to catch the TGV in Bordeaux around lunchtime. I had a dilemma after that... go out with the guys to watch the rugby and forget Celtic's imminent league victory or sit in my room and watch, for the first time, a game on *Rangers Live*. I chose to sit in my room and listen to Gerry McNee.

The game went on and reports came through that Sutton, as expected, had scored midway through the first half - still time to go out and join the boys. *Rangers Live* in those days was still pretty blotchy, but I managed to see Novo hitting the post and thinking that we wouldn't be doing it today. Anyway, Nacho finally scored; meanwhile, Celtic were still only one up - only then I started to think about believing, and not one minute before. I am always the pessimist on these occasions, but was so hopeful I had to go to the loo (No 2). I didn't even bother turning my laptop around so I could watch from my sitting position when I heard that indescribable sound that I had been waiting for (infectious cheering when nothing was happening on the pitch)... I didn't know what to do or think (as long as Well hung in there the league was ours). So the cries of, "Yeeeeesssss," began with the obvious remaining fear of another Celtic goal. Just then, my wife (who doesn't normally watch football, never mind select Setanta on the TV) rang from Paris saying it was 2-1, and I screamed at her that it was still only 1-1 not realising the delay on the internet was so significant. She finally convinced me, then after listening to me screaming like a banshee for a few minutes, hung up.

Only a Hibs equaliser could scupper us now, and it seemed to me that they were happy with the score as the Aberdeen score was going their way - quite happily letting Rangers stroke the ball around the middle of the park (thank you, Hibs, I thought). This was turning into a day that was never envisaged.

As far as the other guests in the hotel were concerned, there must have been a murder taking place in my room... I was delirious, running up and down like an idiot. Celebrating on your own, as anyone else who has done it knows, is strange. I ended up going into downtown Agen in my Rangers top. No one in that famous rugby region had any idea what it was, nor did my colleagues from around Europe who I met there have any idea of my emotions. Only the dozens of international SMS messages between me and my mates (Rangers, Celtic and Hibs fans) could make it real. That was good enough for me - happy days!

Kenneth Stillie

Back on the day that was Helicopter Sunday, I was just 13. My dad's girlfriend had had an operation on her nose and had really bad headaches, so he couldn't watch or listen to the last 20 minutes or thereabouts. After assuming we had lost the league, I had given it up. My dad had thought it was all over too. So I'm sitting in my room, all gloom - when I came up with the idea to listen to some music. So I put the radio on and hear the commentators ranting and raving. From that point I knew something BIG had happened... it could only mean one thing. The helicopter was changing direction.

First instinct was to punch the air and call my dad as he had no clue. When I phoned my dad I can remember clear as day his words, "I was FUCKING hoping that would be you, ya beauty. I'm away to the car to listen to it!" A couple of minutes later I got a call from my dad. "Meet me at Shawlands, we're going to Ibrox".

From then, me, being 13 - with my 2 sisters, 15 and 16 at the time, I ran to Shawlands to meet my dad. We then got a taxi to Ibrox. At Ibrox we waited hours for the team to arrive, and when they did... what an ovation they got. You could tell that everyone in Ibrox that day was in sheer awe at what had happened. I remember fairly vividly Soti Kyrgiakos coming out one of the exits in the Govan Rear stand and waving a Greek flag whilst dancing in his suit. The whole day was brilliant, from that point I knew I had been a part of something so historical. Never have I remembered something so vividly, even all the small details - but that day is unforgettable.

Stuart Mowat

Was in Phnom Phen in Cambodia, nowhere to watch the game so had to follow two min updates on the BBC website. Was typing a depressed e-mail to my brother when the first went in. Let's say that the internet café's collective ears pricked up when I exclaimed, "NO FUCKIN WAY!" at my PC screen. When the second went in, two English guys had to calm me down and explain to the wee Cambodian bloke that I wasn't actually having a fit.

When I finally calmed down enough to speak legibly my only words were: "Telephone. Scotland. I need to phone Scotland," before remembering, heart in mouth, that I needed to check the Hibs-Rangers score.

Phoned everyone I could think of and more, then went

out on the lash… the rest, as they say, is history.

Jonathan Aitken

The day all started by waking up after a restless night's sleep thinking and dreaming of the day ahead. This would be the last game of the season of my 3rd season as a season ticket holder in the Govan Rear. What was about to unfold before my eyes would be the best day of my life ever and will be hard to top.

So me and my dad head down to the Greenock Rangers Supporters club. The club is literally bouncing. Not a seat in sight. Every man who has a connection with Rangers was out to watch us play Hibs and hope upon hope that Motherwell could get a result against 'them'. We sat up the very back of the main hall in the club. A rendition of *Follow, Follow* made the hairs on my neck stand up. I could not imagine what the reaction would be like if we hadn't won the league that day. I remember thinking to myself that this had to be our day.

The amount of people packed into the RSC was unbelievable and people were still coming in after kick-off. The ref blew his whistle and it was just down to us to get through the Hibs game before even thinking about Celtic. News came through that they were 1-0 up and the balloon inside was deflating - the fact we did not have the destiny of the league in our own hands was frustrating to say the least.

Half-time and my dad was telling me that he had stuck a tenner on Rangers to win the league, to tell you the truth I thought he was mad. I was trying to stay positive but with Celtic 1-0 up and we had not scored yet was beginning to get to me. Second half started and the club was still bouncing. I remember us hitting the post and then it finally came, our goal.

We had finally got it, the goal that was needed. "There's only one Nacho Novo," was the chant. 80+ minutes arrived. A tear in my eye was evident - we could not win this league... or could we? A cheer from the TV and the next 2 minutes was a blur. I was standing on top of the seats and the roof was coming in (I still was not sure that Motherwell had equalised or was it the Hibs fans cheering because Aberdeen were getting beat?) We were going mad but now it was obvious that Motherwell had scored.

A party had started. It is a mystery how the Greenock Rangers roof was not completely destroyed. More people were packing into the club. I even saw an old woman with her shopping come in to check out what was happening. Final whistle was blown and the tears of joy from everyone that I looked at was amazing. This is what it was like to be a Bluenose, a Rangers supporter.

The bus steward who had been a Ger all his life came in and hugged me and my dad who was on top of a table at this point (it was obvious the bus steward had not experienced anything like this). This was the most emotional I had ever seen my dad. Three guys started singing, "One Scott McDonald..." what the hell are they talking about, was my initial thoughts.

After an hour of partying I went home to chill out for a bit (or so I thought). My dad took me up to Ibrox where the Rangers supporters were let in to celebrate. There was at least 50,000 supporters on the bottom tiers of the stands. Everyone was celebrating, hugging complete strangers, "Championees, Championees," was ringing in my ears. My emotions were running wild. The guy next to me was telling me that both goals were absolute crackers. Two goals I thought? I asked him what he meant. He said both Scott McDonald's goals. I finally realised who Scott McDonald was. But I did not even know Motherwell had won 2-1. My dad was as surprised as me. We started chanting, "There's only one Scott McDonald".

After the teams came out and did a mini-huddle in front of the Govan we headed home. I remember my afterthought going to bed that night thinking that 2 of the 3 seasons as a season ticket holder were great. In fact they had given me the best days of my life and I can't see anything beating this day.

Helicopter Sunday will be in the hearts of every Rangers supporters until the day we die. 22nd May 2005, a day that will never be forgotten.

"Strangers hugged strangers up and down the land, As the words KEEP BELIEVING appeared in the stand".
WE ARE THE PEOPLE

Stuart MacDonald

There were about 7 of us (me, my mate, my dad and a few of his mates) and we were unsure about what to do as we were all certain they would win the title. We all had the same opinion of, "If they win it, I don't want to be anywhere near the town". As the day approached we decided to go to The Auctioneers pub on St Vincent Street.

The place was packed with fellow Bears and we had a great position right in front of the big screen. As they were winning at Fir Park the first genuine cheer was for Novo's winner at Easter Road. With a few minutes left the place was silent, thinking it was gone. I remember my dad saying to me, "As soon as this is over we're off to the station and getting the first train home!"

During the second half I noticed an old guy, maybe in his 60s, sitting with headphones on listening to the Celtic game about a metre or so away from me. He sat motionless for the entire game and every so often would just say, "It's still 1-0". Then out of the blue with 2 minutes left he said, "There's a goal! It's for Motherwell!"

The whole place went ballistic, guys hugging anyone who was close by. The whole pub had a sense of trepidation as we knew there was still 3 or 4 minutes left. Then the same guy just silenced the whole place and I remember his words to this day, "Ssshh, ssshhh, there's been another goal, it's 2-1 for Motherwell."

That was it, party time, the whole place was dancing and singing to watch the presentation. After that the seven of us proceeded to walk to Ibrox stopping at every Rangers pub on the way for a drink and a sing-song. The traffic stopped on Paisley Road West with a giant bouncy on the way to Ibrox when the team would return with the trophy. Thanks to that old guy in the corner, I never did make that train and I don't know how I got home!

Davy Watson

It was gone, wasn't it? There was no way we could win the league, and despite Marvin telling us all to keep believing, I have to confess I didn't. Sitting at home that Sunday in Cheshire, I was actually toying with the idea of whether to watch the game or not.

On one hand, I didn't want to put myself through the agony that would surely occur by full-time. On the other hand, it was the last game of the season and I wouldn't get a chance to see The Rangers for months. I opted to watch, as the alternative was to help my wife with the household chores.

When the announcement came that Celtic had scored I thought, ach well, that's it then. By half-time, all was going the way most of us thought it would. And whilst I was watching the match, it was more from habit than anything else. When Nacho scored, my first thought was that it would merely result in the season ending on a respectable note - nothing more. As full-time drew nearer, I became aware of something happening amongst the Rangers support, and it seemed to grow and grow, from a rumble to a definite cheer. I was looking at the screen, thinking something had happened off the ball which was not picked up by the cameras. Even the commentator seemed momentarily stunned into silence, as if wondering what could be causing the Rangers support to be roused. He then obviously heard through his earpiece that something had occurred at Fir Park, and the camera turned to the Rangers support. There was obvious confusion, as some supporters were dancing, hugging and cheering, whilst others were frantically looking around, enquiring as to the source of their fellow Bears' joy. When the screen split, and it showed Scott McDonald's goal for Motherwell, I leapt to my feet, and said to my wife, "Naw... this is not possible... is it?"

The message seemed to get through to the Rangers bench, and although some of the players on the pitch looked confused, they were at least professional enough to stroke the ball around, quickly grasping the fact that, should the scores stay as they were, we would be champions. Hibs were content to do the same, in the knowledge that a 0-1 defeat for them would mean they qualified for Europe ahead of Aberdeen.

An agonising minute or two passed, when another rumble and cheer came from the Rangers support. I've seen too many of these turning out to be rumours that spread across terraces like wildfire to be taken in, and although I **wanted** it to be true, I kept my emotions in check. On the touchline, Eck seemed to think it was the final whistle from

Fir Park. Little did he or I know, but future Celtic player Scott McDonald had scored a second, confirmed by the cameras seconds later. That was it for me. Seconds later I was dancing around, safe in the knowledge that, barring a capitulation never before seen, we were champions in the most dramatic of fashions. I phoned my brother, asking him to tell me it wasn't all a dream, and both of us were chattering away so fast we couldn't make out a word the other was saying.

When the final whistle went, I just slumped to my knees, and in the midst of my sheer unadulterated joy, I berated myself for not believing. Marvin Andrews - you have my utmost apologies. If I had a fraction of your faith, I would have believed, and the sight of you looking to the sky at the final whistle will live with me for ever.

Alex Downie

Just moved house in Johannesburg and had no access to e-mail or internet or Sky News. Received a text message that 'they' were one nil up and decided to take the dog for a walk to try and relax as not being able to watch or listen to the game was murder. Then received another text as I was still out with the dog to say we had scored and at least we had kept up our side of what had to be done.

When I got home, my wife could see that I was on edge and we decided to go for another walk in our new neighbourhood. Just as I left the house I received a call to tell me McDonald had scored. My first question was how long to go and the dread that they would benefit from a decision, only to be told that there had been another goal at Fir Park and to great joy and relief the Aussie had scored again. Cue me dancing in the street like a madman far away from Scotland.

Finally got home and sat outside trying to take it all in only to be joined by the wife with a bottle of bubbly. My initial reaction was my wife had kept believing as Marvin had told us, and had the bubbly on ice to celebrate. Only to be told it was to wet the roof in our new home.

Only later when I bought the DVD and the emotion you feel when news come through that the helicopter is turning could I start to feel how it must have felt to be at Easter Road.

Derek Lowe

My wife likes to do her food shopping on a Sunday and as we don't drive my in-laws were taking us to Asda in Helen Street. Shopping is my idea of hell, I hate it with a vengeance and I don't normally go. But the thought of moping around the house for the inevitable to happen, i.e. Celtic winning the league, was depressing me and I decided to tag along.

At that time I didn't have Setanta and a workmate always kept me updated with the score of the Rangers game that was on live. When we left the house Celtic were 1-0 up at Fir Park, Sutton scoring if I remember correctly. Obviously I thought at that point the league was over and was ready for a depressing day traipsing around Asda, or so I thought!

When we finally got to Asda wee Nacho had given us the lead at Easter Road - at least we were doing our bit now, I thought. I had my 8-month-old girl in the trolley and was wandering around with my mobile phone in hand, waiting for Celtic to score their 2nd and put the final nail in our coffin. But as time drew on and I was checking my watch, the 2nd goal hadn't been scored yet.

Time was passing by and my mobile still hadn't rung. By this time there was around 3 minutes to go and I was thinking if Celtic haven't scored again they'll be getting very nervous as they hadn't killed Motherwell off.

I decided to text my mate to see what, if anything, had happened - he text back saying nothing had changed, both of the Old Firm were 1-0 up. I still thought Celtic were going to hold out but knew they'd be bricking it as it was getting very near the end of the game and if Well scored they were in deep trouble.

A couple of minutes later I thought I could hear a commotion up one of the aisles and then one of the most wonderful phone calls I've received came through. My mate was shouting down the phone, "Motherwell have fucking scored!"

I replied, "Willie, don't wind me up please."

"I'm not," he replied. "We're going to win the bloody league."

While I was on the phone one of my other mates text me asking where I was.

By this time my wife and in-laws saw me going mental - apparently my face was chalk white, people were coming up to me asking what was happening and all I could say was, "I don't believe it, we're going to win the league."

I phoned my mate telling him I was in Asda and knew what was happening he told me there was 1 minute injury time and said he would call back at the final whistle - I was still nervous thinking they would equalise. I was just about to put my phone in my pocket when my mate rang again. The first thing I thought was they had equalised and was ready to go crazy with disappointment. But when he spoke it was hard to make out it was a garbled sound and I could just about hear him say, "2-1 Motherwell!"

The feeling was indescribable it was one of total elation, all I could say, or should it be shout, was, "WE'VE WON THE LEAGUE!"

It goes without saying I had attracted a lot of attention - my wife had taken the trolley with our little girl as I was otherwise engaged so to speak! Folk were asking what was going on and I told them with great delight that Rangers were the Champions.

I'll always remember seeing a guy with a Celtic top on and looking at me with disbelief that his team had blown it big style.

The next 4 hours or more when I finally got home I was in a daze and couldn't sit down for any length of time. And God knows how much I spent on phone calls and text messages but it was worth it for one of the best days of my life.

Unfortunately I didn't make it to Ibrox but it was still a memorable day.

Keith Orr

My first thought of the day was when I woke up and I put the radio on and heard that Proclaimers song, *Sunshine on Leith*.

A couple of hours later the Willie Waddell No1 travel club got together in my house with a few Buds. There was no bus this week as it blew up on the way to Ibrox the week before at the Harthill service station. There were 9 of us and only 8 tickets and 4 cars. One of our guys, Jamie, said that he had a ticket from the season before and he would go and get it. He brought it back and lo and behold it was just a lighter shade of tan from this day's ticket. So the decision was made for young Lee to take it and off we went to Easter Road not knowing what would happen.

We parked the cars on Regent Road and walked down together. We got to the turnstiles and the police were checking all tickets. So we bunched together and one of the guys passed his ticket to Lee to show the police. After he had shown it, we got through - next the turnstiles. Me and Doc had Lee between us and said we'll push him if there was any hassle. We got to the gate and it was an old guy who looked like Harry Potter with the specs on. Lee got through with no probs, happy days.

At half-time I had two blue smoke bombs and lit them and threw them down. The police and stewards were right up at the rows we were in, but we got away with that. Then the final last couple of minutes, Doc brought out the bookie's slip with a tenner on Motherwell at 11/1. We then went totally bananas when the news came through. We were dancing with delight and showing the bookie's slip to anyone who would look as we had not a jot of dough between us.

After the chaos of the celebration we made our way back to the car with the winning line. A couple of young Hibs neds saw us with it and made their way over shouting abuse and it seemed they wanted the slip. At that two policeman on horses came to the rescue (unbelievable).

We made our way along Princes Street, stopping at the traffic lights and getting out and doing the bouncy. We got to the Haymarket and I made the car do circles till I picked the bet up from the Ladbrokes there. Then it was off to The Tap Shop in Mid Calder, where the landlord let us into the restaurant (which was closed) to drink and sing to our hearts' content.

Stevie Bachelor/Richard Reid

My mate picked me up and we headed to Shawlands to watch the game - he was driving as he didn't think we had a chance - I had a wee funny feeling something might happen! Arriving in Shawlands we find most pubs showing the scum game but The Corona was showing the Gers - watched the first half in there. At half-time we decided to head up to an old Gers pub Finlays - and it turned out it wasn't such a Gers pub anymore as they showed the game at Fir Park. Back down to the Corona and still my mate wasn't for having a drink.

Second half started and then Novo scores. Pub erupts but we're still waiting for Motherwell to do us a turn. Time is ticking by and then someone shouts, "Motherwell have scored!"

Pub is in silence as we don't know to believe him or not. Then the screen swaps to Fir Park and then the ball hits the net and everybody goes wild. And then we are praying for the final whistle. Screen cuts to Fir Park again and we aren't sure what's happening next when McDonald hits it and I've never hugged and kissed so many men before in my life. Final whistle at Easter Road, cue bar staff all up on the bar spraying champagne over everyone in the pub. Obviously at this point my mate says, "Fuck it, car's getting dumped - I'll get a taxi to work tomorrow!"

The feeling when Motherwell scored their second will live with me for ever and has only been matched by that penalty against Fiorentina.

Jim Guthrie

My fiancée until quite recently, her uncle is one of UK's top psychics. On the Saturday her brother told me he had spoken to the uncle and he had predicted Arsenal to win the FA Cup, Rangers to win the League and Liverpool the Champions League. He was going to bet £1000 on this.

Anyway, Arsenal duly won on penalties in a game dominated by Man United. Fate? Come Sunday we were watching our niece and I had decided to go to a garden centre as I had no hope of us winning and couldn't bring myself to watch. Popped in to drop the niece off and the Dhims were one up and us at nil-nil. Couldn't bring myself to watch the second half but her face was tripping her and I stayed and watched it. When Motherwell equalised, I nearly fainted and when the second went in we went berserk. She thought I was going to have a heart attack!

Anyway, it turns out her brother has put £500 on the treble and still needs Liverpool to win the Champions League. My best mate at my London-based company was off to the Final the following week, he is a Liverpool season ticket holder. He phoned me on the Monday to congratulate me and I told him about the psychic's predictions.

After what had happened I felt confident. Until half-time in the CL final that is. "Fucking psychics," we were saying. But it got back to 3-3 and the rest is history and her brother won £15,200 on his treble.

Stuart Barr

Living in Dubai, this was the hardest day I ever had being away from home as I was devastated I wasn't at the game (been going to the games at home since I was three and to away games and Europe since I was 11). I used to be a member of the Govan True Blues and I am now a member of the Kinning Park Loyal.

The game was being shown in Biggles Bar at the

Millennium Airport hotel (where the Dubai Loyal used to meet, and some still do). On the big screen as you come in the door we had the Bears game on and in the corner on the small telly, the tims game. I guess there were only around 30-35 of us in for the start of the game. You see, it being a hotel near the airport, it's full of people from all over the world on a quick stopover, so it can be hard to judge. Anyway, after the Bears scored, there were some good celebrations but slightly muted as we knew we still needed results elsewhere. As the game progressed we realised that our game seemed to be a formality, I reckon 95% of us started watching (or praying whilst doing so!) the Celtic game on the other telly for the last 20 mins.

Whilst we were all sinking the pints and, to be honest, more or less crying into them, everyone of us to a man had the same idea. PLEASE MOTHERWELL, PLEASE. Then it happened.

As that goal went in, I'm sure you could have heard us in Glasgow, the place went berserk! Drink flying everywhere, men kissing each other, people on tables, not to mention the odd Arab/Yank tourist looking at us all as if we were madmen!

As the second went in, I genuinely had tears in my eyes. I just couldn't believe it. FULL-TIME: again, madness and then a full sash-up began as the place was rocking. As the time went on, more Bears who had been in other pubs across the city began to come in and it was party time. Champagne out, and I'm on to top of a table giving it laldy. And then this American guy says to me, "Did the Rangers win?"

I said. "No mate, we got fucked! What do you think?"

As guys started falling off stools, hammering shots etc. etc. hard to remember who was all there at the start of the game. But guys/girls who were all there as the night progressed include my girlfriend Laura Nibloe, Grant Douglas, Norrie McDonald, Mike Smith, Craig Miller, Jim the teacher, Jim McCloy, Craig McCloy (the McCloys are related to Peter McCloy) and many others.

As the night progressed, I became slightly the worse for wear. Laura was enjoying the festivities when I said I would be back in a minute. Sensing I was bladdered, she followed me out to see me outside the hotel, being sick after drinking vodka, champagne, lager, brandy and Christ knows what else that night. After throwing up I casually said, "Right let's get wasted," and at that point I was bundled into a taxi and taken home by Laura.

But what a night and I'll always remember it.

Steven ma

Was one of the lucky ones who got a ticket for the game through my supporters club. My RSC got 2 tickets which were allocated to me and my mate Willie McKinven as we were at the top of the points system. The tickets were for the top tier of the Whyte & Mackay stand and I still have the ticket stub to this day.

After about 10 minutes the Hibs keeper made a mistake and left the goal open and Novo hit the post. About half an hour or so into the game I heard a cheer from the Hibs end and I knew that 'they' had scored. It didn't seem like it was going to be our day.

As there were no scoreboards at Easter Road, I lost track of time so I raised my arm and pulled back my jacket to check my watch to see roughly how long was left. It was 3:50pm. That's it, they've won it now, their game must be about over, I thought, as I resigned myself to the fact that we would not win the league. As I lowered my arm, a large cheer arose and the whole stand erupted in sheer unadulterated bedlam. Willie was trying to listen in on his radio to see what had happened at Fir Park but the noise was so great he couldn't hear. It became clear after a minute that this wasn't a hoax or a false alarm and that Motherwell had in fact equalised. My feelings were more of disbelief and shock than jubilation. I was convinced that this was too good to be true and that 'they' would score a late winner like they always seem to do.

A second loud cheer erupted which I believed to have marked the final whistle at Fir Park. A few seconds later the whistle goes in our game and the Rangers bench runs onto the pitch to celebrate. I then receive a phone call from my dad who tells me that Motherwell have scored again and I held my mobile aloft so he could hear the crowd celebrating. I now felt elated and on top of the world knowing that Rangers had won the league in the most dramatic fashion possible. It's the best feeling I've ever had watching Rangers and I was buzzing for days afterwards due to me being on such a high.

On the bus home we were caught in traffic lights in Port Glasgow across from Coronation Park, where some of the Port Tims were drowning their sorrows. One big fat Tim spots the bus and runs 50 yards toward the bus, collapsing 3 times before summoning the strength to throw his can of super at the bus, missing it by miles. Unsurprisingly the resulting cheer on the bus was not quite as loud as the cheers when Motherwell scored though.

A.McCombe

The 3 of us usually went to away games together. Me, my dad and my uncle. Unfortunately only my uncle and I had tickets and my dad was hoping to get a ticket from the supporters bus. We got on the bus and the bus convener told my dad he'd have to wait to see if there was a ticket. So obviously my dad was panicking and so nervous. He wasn't going to go to the game at all but he said he had a feeling that he had to be there. I was shocked he felt like that as I didn't think for a minute we could pull it off and the only reason I was going was for the day out and to see the Rangers for the last time that season. I very nearly gave my dad my ticket as my father-in-law was in hospital dying with cancer and the family had been called to the hospital the day before. But he'd rallied and my other half told me to go to the game and try to have fun. So off we went.

The bus journey was entertaining, loads of singing, people optimistic, but more people very pessimistic – me included. Then as we neared Edinburgh someone started singing, "You're never gonna believe us, we're gonna win the league."

Aye right, I thought with a smile on my face, in our dreams!

My dad got his ticket from the bus and in the pub before the game he just had a big grin on his face like a five-year-old at Christmas and kept saying, "I can feel something here, something's going to happen." We just humoured him.

I felt the tension around me as the game went on. Celtic scored, the Hibs fans slagged us for that. Then Novo scored and after we'd all calmed down it was pretty much everyone saying, "Well at least we've done what we needed to do."

The game went on and it was obvious we were settling for 1-0 and Hibs were settling for the same. Then absolute bedlam. I didn't know what had happened, then heard Motherwell had scored! Oh my God, could Motherwell hold on? There were scenes of joy then panic as people thought, c'mon, Celtic usually score in the last minute they'll equalise.

I tried to listen to the radio on my phone but couldn't hear a thing as there was so much noise. People hugging total strangers, singing, dancing, phoning their mates and family to find out how long to go at Fir Park. The next thing another almighty roar. My uncle and I collapsed in each others arms, we didn't know whether the game was finished or what had happened. Then we heard Motherwell had scored again. I was still panicking in case the officials added on so much time that Celtic scored 2 – we can't be this lucky, I kept thinking. Eventually we got the news that the game was over, we'd won the league! Motherwell had done it!

The scenes at Easter Road will live with me for ever, grown men crying and hugging each other, fans running on the pitch, the sheer joy on the faces of the players as they came running back out the tunnel. We just wanted to be there on the pitch with them, all celebrating together.

The celebrations lasted forever it seemed and even walking out of Easter Road stadium you met even more people you knew and hugged them (and sometimes people you didn't know!) The walk back to the buses and more hugs and kisses as you all met there.

Our bus stopped in Harthill on the way home and what a reception we got in the local pub there. I don't think any of us bought a drink all night, the lovely people there saw to it that our glasses were never empty.

After a few refreshments there we began the journey home, and on the way home we drove along Paisley Road West and that was a sight to behold. Full of flags, Rangers supporters all singing and dancing in the streets, people standing outside pubs raising their glasses to our bus. We passed Ibrox and the crowds were just beginning to disperse and there were thousands of Bears - men, women and kids - all around and all with huge smiles on their faces.

Finally we arrived home and greeted our families who had watched the game on TV and the champagne was opened.

The day, however, was tinged with sadness, in all the sheer joy and partying, my father-in-law's family had all been called back to the hospital, where his condition was deteriorating. I felt guilty because I couldn't be there to support them and because of the fact that I'd been out celebrating while they were all so upset. I got my chance to say goodbye to him the next day and I often wonder if he held on to see the Rangers win the league.

The next day I was up at the crack of dawn, going to the newsagents to buy every single paper there was, and then back home to watch the game again. I think since that day I've watched the game loads of times and listened to the commentary from the radio several times as well – 'the Helicopter is changing direction' is a saying that will live with us all for ever.

Epilogue

My quandary when putting together this book was how to end it. It has always seemed a bit abrupt. Last tale – book end.

So the events leading up to the end of the recent (2008/09) League season presented the answer. In the week leading up to the final day showdown this year, the pilot of the helicopter on that momentous day in 2005 was traced by the Daily Record. After a few enquiries an e-mail was swiftly fired of to John McKenzie who agreed to speak to me and share his memories.

John is a Manchester United supporter, but is a lapsed Aberdeen supporter from Dingwall and says he is really an Alex Ferguson fan. In spite of all this he is a thoroughly decent chap. John is a very experienced pilot and served nine years in the Army. He has also flown all manner of celebrities and dignitaries, including members of the Royal Family and Kofi Annan.

Currently he does a lot of work for Air Ambulance and a donation from the proceeds of the book will go towards this. My own aunt made use of these services a few years ago.

On that Sunday in 2005 he carried the crown jewels of the Scottish game. The helicopter was based for the day at Cumbernauld and with about fifteen minute of the game to go they took off and headed towards Strathclyde Park. After being in the air for around ten minutes they had to change plans dramatically as events unfolded and the green and white ribbons were torn from the trophy and left lying on the chopper floor. Interestingly, they did not actually change direction till after the second goal.

While John would not give too much away he said the

indecent haste with which the green and grey ribbons were ripped from the trophy indicated the helicopter occupants were not entirely unhappy with how events unfolded.

It was then a mad dash following the track of the M8 to the grounds of the Prestonfield Hotel at the foot of Arthur's Seat and then Howard from Bank of Scotland, Lex Gold et al jumped into a waiting car to deliver the trophy to the eager hands of Fernando Ricksen.

John got to deliver the trophy to the righteous this year again, but last year was not on duty. So if we get a close finish in the future we Bears know the way to success - have John McKenzie literally in the driving seat.